THE HERO HANDBOOK

To the three wise women of my life, Megan, Karen, and Vienna for influencing me every day.

To Michelle, whose unstoppable force continues to drive me.

And to the hundreds of people I've met on this "hero-stuff" journey.

—ML

Copyright © 2021 by Magination Press, an imprint of the American Psychological Association. All rights reserved. Except as permitted under the United States Copyright Act of 1976, no part of this publication may be reproduced or distributed in any form or by any means, or stored in a database or retrieval system, without the prior written permission of the publisher.

Magination Press is a registered trademark of the American Psychological Association. Order books at maginationpress.org, or call 1-800-374-2721.

Book design by Rachel Ross and Circle Graphics, Inc., Reisterstown, MD
Cover printed by Phoenix Color, Hagerstown, MD
Interior printed by Sheridan Books, Inc., Chelsea, MI
Check Out the Science! by Brian Riches

Library of Congress Cataloging-in-Publication Data
Names: Langdon, Matt, author.
Title: The hero handbook / Matt Langdon.
Description: Washington, DC : Magination Press, [2021] | Summary:
   "To become a hero, kids can surround themselves with supportive people,
   boost their self-esteem and self-awareness, find their passion, and have the
   courage make things happen"—Provided by publisher.
Identifiers: LCCN 2020033210 (print) | LCCN 2020033211 (ebook) |
   ISBN 9781433827969 (hardcover) | ISBN 9781433834332 (ebook)
Subjects: LCSH: Heroes—Juvenile literature. | Courage—Juvenile literature.
Classification: LCC BJ1533.H47 L36 2021 (print) | LCC BJ1533.H47 (ebook) |
   DDC 170/.44—dc23
LC record available at https://lccn.loc.gov/2020033210
LC ebook record available at https://lccn.loc.gov/2020033211

Manufactured in the United States of America
10 9 8 7 6 5 4 3 2 1

THE HERO HANDBOOK

BY MATT LANGDON

Magination Press • Washington, DC
American Psychological Association

TABLE OF CONTENTS

PREFACE

So you want to be a hero?

Or maybe you're not sure. What does that even mean, anyway? Well, we'll talk about it. But this book is for anyone looking to find a little more direction—whether that means setting some goals and coming up with a plan for your own life, or just means learning how to affect some change in your community. Or the world! This book is going to help you figure out how to be someone who takes action instead of standing by, and who works to move their own journey forward.

I'm going to take you on that journey—through some journeys. Hero journeys. We'll talk about what

a hero's journey looks like in stories (from myths to movies), and what it looks like in real life. We'll talk about what makes a hero: the steps, the people, the goals, and the powers. And we'll talk about how you can be the hero of your own story. (It shouldn't need to be said, but in case it does: we're not going to talk about any differences between "hero" or "heroine"—because there aren't any. A hero can be anyone, and it's silly to act like there are two different things because of sex or gender.)

Throughout the book, you'll find some "Check out the science!" boxes by psychologist Brian Riches, who will explain the science behind some of the concepts I'm talking about (in case you don't want to just take my word for it). Believe it or not, there are psychological studies to back up what I'm telling you about heroes!

Each chapter ends with a quick sum-up of the key points, but if you want to write down some of your own ideas, reactions, and plans as you go along, go ahead! I won't tell you to "take notes" (that sounds too much like schoolwork), but you might want to jot down your thoughts. Or you might not. You do you. There are also several activities and prompts to get you started on your own journey, and I do think you should do those—that's kind of the point! Plus, they should be fun.

Warning: Heroes take risks. The best risks are those you've thought about. You'll read about people who jumped onto train tracks, stood up to bullies, and changed the world. It might make sense for you to take a particular risk, but it might not. Each person's riskiness is unique. Trying to save a drowning kid in the ocean might be low-risk for a lifeguard, but for me it's very high-risk. This book is going to challenge you to take risks, but before every one, I want you to evaluate the risk to you first.

And before we start, since I'm about to give you a bunch of life advice, I guess it's only fair that I tell you who I am. What makes me qualified to tell you about heroes? I'm Matt. I started the Hero Construction Company, an organization that helps come up with plans to teach people to act heroically. I'm also a member of groups like the Hero Round Table and the Heroic Imagination Project. My job literally consists of speaking all over the world, telling people how to be heroes. How's that for qualifications?

Ready? Let's go!

CHAPTER 1

WHAT IS THE HERO'S JOURNEY?

Who is your hero?

I wonder who just popped into your head. Who's sitting there, grinning back at you? Is it a famous person, like Martin Luther King, Jr. or Ruth Bader Ginsburg? Is it a superhero from a comic or movie? Is it an athlete, artist, or accountant inspiring you to great things? If you're like most people your age, it's a family member: a parent, sibling, or other relative who is always there for you.

It's a strange question because I didn't give you a definition. I didn't lead you in a particular direction by adding more information. I didn't ask who the greatest hero in history was. I didn't ask for the name of a family hero. I left it broad.

It's a powerful question. When someone provides an answer to this question, you can tell a lot about them. You get an idea of what motivates them, what their values are, what they value in others, and even what their interests are. What could you gather about someone who said Spiderman was their hero? You could assume they're a superhero fan, generally. It might be safe to say they value responsibility, due to Spidey's famous tagline. They might feel unpopular, feeling a connection to Peter Parker's life of school nerd. They probably have a strong sense of justice and like to support the underdog. Compare that with someone who tells you their hero is Anne Frank, or Nelson Mandela, or Simone Biles, or their mother.

Go and ask an adult in your life who their hero is and who held the title when they were your age. Yes, I mean now. I know you're barely a couple of pages into the book, but read the Hero Interview below, put the book down and go ask them. It's going to help get you in the right frame of mind. And it's going to give you an insider look into what makes that person tick.

HERO INTERVIEW!

You are going to find out about the heroes of an adult in your life. They might be your parents, or your coach, or your aunt Jessyca. You're going to do this because someone's hero says a lot about them. Before you start the interview, you need to come up with some interview questions.

The two basic questions are: Who was your hero as a child? and Who is your hero now? You can create a set of questions to expand their knowledge of the two heroes. Write the list down if you want—make this interview official! Here are some ideas to get you started:

When was your hero born?
Where was your hero from?
Why were they your hero?
What did your hero do for a living?

Welcome back. I imagine you just had an interesting conversation. One thing that may have come up is the definition of the word hero. It's pretty clear by the different types of answers that it's *not* quite clear. Is it possible that the average parent falls under the same definition as Gandhi? Does Gandhi fit in with a firefighter? Do firefighters have the same attributes as professional sports players?

This uncertainty means I need to start a hero-training book with some definition building. There's not much point in explaining how to be a hero if we're talking about two different things.

WHAT IS A HERO?

It would be traditional to start a conversation about definition by quoting a dictionary. This is not a traditional book, so I'm not going to do that. Plus, that's boring. And dictionaries are not very useful in this case. Suffice to say, dictionaries often say a hero has done famous things (not usually) or is a sandwich (technically correct).

We could look to the media to help us work out what a hero is. Just kidding. News networks and sports reporters use the word like it's a headline magic trick. It's not heroic to hit the winning run. It's not heroic to play a sport with an injury. It's not heroic to do your job. And it's not heroic to die because you were in the wrong place at the wrong time.

You might think history could provide some insight. Unfortunately, history is where the dictionary got its information. One hundred years ago a hero was someone who killed lots of people in war. A couple of hundred years before that it was someone who conquered countries. Two thousand years ago, a hero was half-god. That's not really something you can aspire to—having a god as a parent just comes down to luck.

Speaking of gods, though, that leads me to mythology. Is there something there for us to latch onto? In myth and story, the hero offers us an example of how to live our lives. The hero is an exemplar—literally a good example. That helps explain why battlefield triumph was so important for so long—war was an important (and unavoidable) part of life. It also explains why we have so much trouble pinning down a definition in today's world. There are so many of us, living in different cultures, but also living in each other's pockets on our phones, that there's no way we could all agree on what a good example is.

Mythology and stories will let me get started on my efforts to define "hero" for you, though. So, let's begin.

DEFINITION 1: THE HERO IN A STORY

The first definition of "hero" that I'm going to explore is this: a hero is the main character of a story. That's pretty non-confrontational. Everyone can agree with that, I think. When you read a book, watch a movie, or otherwise consume a story, the main character is called the hero.

Back in 1949, a man named **Joseph Campbell** wrote a book called *The Hero With a Thousand Faces*. He had spent the previous decade traveling the world reading and listening to stories about heroes from mythology. Sounds like a great job, right? I need to get that job.

Campbell noticed that all of these stories were basically the same. No matter when the story was created, where it was told, or who told it, the story was always the same. Now, that sounds a bit crazy. You've seen and read hundreds of stories—they weren't all the same, right? He wasn't saying that they're exactly the same, though. He was saying that they all have the same pattern. A hero from two thousand years ago in the

Middle East has the same basic steps in their story as a hero from two hundred years ago in England and the one in a movie coming out this weekend in India.

Campbell called this pattern the "Hero's Journey."

Let's pause to consider a couple of stories that you might be familiar with.

Story One: Set in a world with humans, elves, and dwarves, a ring of great power is discovered. This golden ring makes the wearer invisible and creates in them a strong desire to hold onto the ring forever. A group of companions set out to destroy the ring. The group is led by a man descended from kings who lives anonymously in the woods. An old, broken sword is re-forged in an effort to defeat the evil creator of the ring. The ring ends up being destroyed by taking it back to where it was created.

Story Two: A young boy in London grows up with his aunt and uncle. He wears glasses and has hard-to-control hair. One day a group of magicians tell him that he is destined to be the greatest wizard to have ever lived. They show him that there is a magical world existing right alongside our own normal world. He befriends an owl and begins to learn magic.

I'm sure you recognized the stories. One is Wagner's "Ring Cycle" and the other is Neil Gaiman's "The Books of Magic" series about a boy named Tim Hunter. That's what you guessed, right?

There are no new stories, just new versions of stories. They (very nearly) all fit the pattern that Joseph Campbell laid out in his book. The Hero's Journey is present in every story. You can see the steps if you know what to look for.

Campbell wrote down these steps. He came up with about 40. Some stories miss a few, while some contain them all. Now, I could tell you about each of those 40 steps in this book, but you'd probably fall asleep or hate me forever. Maybe both. So, I have reduced it to five basic steps that every hero story contains. You're welcome.

The steps are:
1. Mundane World
2. Call to Adventure
3. Threshold
4. Path of Trials
5. Master of Two Worlds

The hero begins the story in the **Mundane World**. Mundane means normal, typical, or boring. The hero doesn't want to be there, but often they don't know how to get out or even what else is available to them. This is Luke Skywalker's Tatooine, Dorothy's Kansas, and Frodo's Shire. It's also T'Challa's Wakanda and Katniss's District 12.

At some point, early in the story, the hero receives a **Call to Adventure**. This is usually someone (or something) that tells the hero that there is something else out there—that they don't have to stay in the Mundane World. It could be an invitation to attend Hogwarts or join the Rebel Alliance. It could be a tornado, a bite from a radioactive spider, or inheriting a magical ring.

Once the hero decides to enter this new world, they have to cross a **Threshold**. A threshold can be thought of as a doorway or gate. The threshold sits between the old world and the new world. Sometimes it's a simple step like Dorothy stepping out the front door of her house that has recently arrived in Oz, Mulan entering the army camp for training, or Katniss getting on the train to the Capitol. Often there is a test for the hero before they can pass.

Upon entering the new world, the hero travels along the **Path of Trials**. This path is full of new people, challenges, and lessons. The hero meets friends, enemies, and **mentors**.

They have to overcome tests of various types, and they start gaining new wisdom. This step is usually the bulk of the story (it often seems like a whole journey itself, not just a step!). Sometimes the path is literal, like the Yellow Brick Road. Sometimes the friends are obvious, like Katara and Sokka. Sometimes the enemies are purely wicked, like Sauron. Sometimes the lessons are clearly stated, like "with great power comes great responsibility." Sometimes they're not.

At the end of the journey, the hero has changed. The new people, tests, and knowledge have all combined to alter the hero forever. That brings the hero to the final step—the **Master of Two Worlds**. Upon surviving the new world, the hero has mastered it. They then return to the old world as a changed person. Because they've changed, they start changing the world around them. Notice that when T'Challa's story ends, he returns to the throne of Wakanda, but it's clear that the country will never be the same. Wakanda changes its priorities according to what T'Challa learned on his journey. An outreach center is built and Wakanda makes its presence known to the world. T'Challa's journey has changed him and thus Wakanda and the entire world changes too.

There are millions of stories in the world. Billions, really. Are the main characters of each of those stories a hero? They are, according to the first definition. That's not great—it doesn't solve the problem of trying to work out what a hero is. The word hero means something narrower. We need something better.

Naturally, that leads us to penguins. Well, one penguin in particular. Mumble Happy Feet. There's a great line in the movie *Happy Feet* that can act as a definition of a hero. After nearing the end of his Path of Trials, Mumble decides to leap off a giant ice cliff to pursue a ship. It's a huge decision for the little penguin who can't sing, as he's risking his life on the hope that the ship will lead him to a solution to the problems of the penguin colonies. His mentor, Lovelace, is duly impressed and yells out after him, "I'm gonna be telling your story, Happy Feet, long after you're dead and gone!"

Lovelace is saying that a hero is someone whose story gets told. Everyone has their own story, but a hero's story gets shared far and wide. What makes a story shareable? Why tell Mumble's story instead of one of the other penguins? It's because there is a lesson in it for us.

Pauline McLeod, an Australian Aboriginal storyteller, explained this. "You can be a yarnteller—telling about something that may or may not have happened down the street or in the community—but it lacks the lessons. The true role of the storyteller is to pass on the lessons from the beginning of time."

We tell stories that help make us better people. A hero is someone whose story has lessons for us.

DEFINITION 2: EVERYDAY HEROES

There is still room for confusion on that definition though. We tell the stories of Babe Ruth, Martin Luther King, Jr., and the woman who runs into a burning building to save a stranger. We use those stories because we want people to achieve great things, to have a mission, and to be selfless. But those three people are not very similar.

To me, there are three different types of everyday heroes. It's this that causes much of the confusion. So let's try to un-confuse the situation by exploring the categories of heroes.

1. The Idol: Achievement and Fame

The **Idol** acts as an inspiration. Through achievement and the subsequent fame, the Idol provides a goal for us. We see what they did and want to replicate it. We want to be them or be like them. Inspirational people play an important role in our lives. The Idol is typically the type of hero provided when you ask someone, "who is your hero?"

Amelia Earhart spent most of her adult life breaking aviation records. Altitude by a woman, crossing the Atlantic by a woman, and so on. Her story is filled with courage, achievement, and mystery, with a generous dash of feminist appeal. There's no surprise that she is a hero to many. She is an idol. Just like LeBron James, Alexandria Ocasio-Cortez, and Ferris Bueller (Idols can be fictional, too).

2. The Action Hero: Fixing a Problem Over Time

The **Action Hero** sees a problem, creates a solution, and then executes it. This happens over time and it changes the world. The keyword for the Action Hero is sacrifice. News outlets love Action Heroes. Every year CNN holds an awards ceremony at the end of the year in which they recognize Action Heroes (they just call them CNN Heroes) from around the world as submitted by their viewers. These people are changing their worlds through action and sacrifice.

Madison Stewart is known as Shark Girl. She grew up on the northeast coast of Australia, spending most of her time in or near the water. When she realized that her underwater home was changing drastically, she decided to do something. Feeling a kinship with the sharks, who are so misunderstood, she started to campaign against the indiscriminate killing of them as a perceived risk and their systematic slaughter as a food source. Using her camera, Madison began filming the sharks in the water and, on land, campaigning to raise awareness of their plight. In 2017, she was named Young Conservationist of the Year.

Madison Stewart is an Action Hero. She sacrificed her time and money to fix a problem.

3. The Reaction Hero: Split-Second Decision Making

The **Reaction Hero** sees a problem and has to act immediately to fix it. There's no time to plan or contemplate options. It's now or never. The keyword for the Reaction Hero is risk.

Wesley Autrey was waiting in a subway station with his two daughters, aged four and six. He saw a 19-year-old man fall onto the tracks. With little time to consider his actions he jumped down from the platform to help. Getting the man up was not easy and before he was successful, he saw the train coming. Instead of jumping up to the platform to save himself and be with his girls, he placed the man between the tracks and lay on top of him to protect him from the train. Six cars of the train ran over them without touching anything but Autrey's hat. (When the train stopped, he yelled up to make sure his daughters knew that he was okay, since seeing your dad get run over by a train tends to be a little traumatic.) Autrey risked his life to save someone else.

The Carnegie Awards focus on Reaction Heroes. Every year they recognize the people who rescued strangers from blazing fires, raging rivers, and speeding trains.

With three different types of heroes, it is easy to understand where some of the confusion comes from. If I'm telling you my idea of a hero is Angelina Jolie and you're thinking about Reaction Heroes, you might think I'm nuts. Likewise, if you tell me your hero is Neil Armstrong and I'm expecting an Action Hero, I might be disappointed.

NO ONE IS PERFECT

In times gone by, heroes were mythical. Thousands of years ago, they were actually mythical like Anansi and Hel. Hundreds of years ago, they just seemed that way. The average person never expected to meet a hero. No one really expected to be able to shake the hand of Joan of Arc or Robert the Bruce.

They certainly didn't think they deserved to know something as personal as what either of them had for breakfast.

Fast forward to the modern world, where breakfast details are fair game. The shrinking of the world through the advances in communications and computers has changed things for heroes. Not only are the positive stories of world-changers talked about, so are their mundane and negative activities. Our brave new world has made it virtually impossible to pretend to be anything but yourself.

So now each of us is confronted with the humanity of our heroes. They're all real people. Would your hero still have the title if you found out that they smoke? What about if they make money from their heroism? What if they say something racist?

Let's look at three famous heroes and some of the claims against them.

George Washington: Owned slaves. Had lots of military failures. Made a lot of money by being president.

Mother Teresa: Was hypocritical on divorce. Fought against women's rights. Hid millions of dollars in donations.

Mohandas Gandhi: Was often cruel to those around him and regularly racist.

What are we supposed to do with this sort of information? That's tough reading for someone who lists these people as personal heroes.

Human frailty has to be accepted as we look for heroes. It's a fact of life. So, how do we balance it? Is there a golden ratio of good versus bad that we can apply to each of our hero candidates? It would be nice to have a hero scale so we can simply add up each of the good things (weighted, of course) and subtract the bad. A net positive results in heroism. Yay. Or maybe it's a ratio—1.618 good things for every bad. Beat the ratio and you have a hero.

Unfortunately, it's not that simple. Every hero's status is subjective according to the viewer. The negatives and positives are weighed up in the individual observer's mind. In that mind lies all of the biases from childhood upbringing, cultural lens, religion, access to facts, and personal experiences. My opinions and your reasons can both be valid as long as we can explain how we balanced the good with the bad.

So, in the modern world, where you can find out what your hero is having for breakfast, remember that as long as you can explain why a person is heroic to you and justify any negative points, they get to have the title.

In his book, *The Tipping Point,* Malcolm Gladwell has some great thoughts about character—such an important part of heroism.

"Character, then, isn't what we think it is or, rather, what we want it to be. It isn't a stable, easily identifiable set of closely related traits, and it only seems that way because of a glitch in the way our brains are organized. Character is more like a bundle of habits and tendencies and interests, loosely bound together and dependent, at certain times, on circumstance and context. The reason that most of us seem to have a consistent character is that most of us are really good at controlling our environment."
—Malcolm Gladwell, *The Tipping Point*

Gladwell says that he likes dinner parties, and his friends think he's fun—so he throws lots of dinner parties. That is a controlled environment. He admits he may not be so fun in other situations, like on the bus, or while running a marathon.

This theory goes a long way to explaining the general idea that heroes are never perfect. There's always something a critic can throw up to attempt to discredit someone. Mother Teresa, George Washington, and Mohandas Gandhi all have their detractors. Perhaps we should always be describing the situation in which the hero has become heroic.

Mother Teresa is considered heroic for her dedication to helping the poor and the "untouchable," but she is criticized for many of her financial dealings and her opinions on women's rights. She was able to control her environment to a great extent, so she was able to remain "heroic" and "caring" in the public eye. It simply doesn't make sense in our heads that someone could be caring and also greedy. That is due to our need for simplicity; to label someone with a character trait, just as Malcolm Gladwell is labeled "fun" by the friends he hosts at his dinner parties.

So, when we're calling someone a hero we need to remember that we are simplifying to keep our brain happy. We're not ignoring flaws. We're not looking for a perfect, shining example. We are describing the actions of someone in a certain environment or situation and seeing heroism.

PUT ON YOUR OWN MASK

If you've been on a plane, you will have heard this line: "If you are travelling with a child or someone who requires assistance, secure your own mask first, and then assist the other person." They tell us this because parents and caregivers are quick to help. The problem is that if you don't get your own

CHECK OUT THE SCIENCE!
Judgment and Attribution Errors

A person's behavior is caused by either an internal cause (like a personality trait or talent) or an external cause (like the situation or environment at the time). **Attribution theory** is about how we think about the causes of other people's behavior. Most often we assume a person's behavior is because of an internal factor—that person is just mean, or always grumpy. But of course, situations can really affect our behavior! Like maybe the person is tired that day, and with more sleep their behavior would be totally different. When we judge heroes' behaviors, we can weigh the choices they made in their lives, thinking carefully about what causes we attribute to their behaviors. Were their behaviors caused by an internal or external cause? Were they in control of the situation or did they not really have much (or any!) control? Thinking about these questions, and how they compare to our own **moral values,** can help us decide if someone is a hero.

mask sorted out first, you're going to have an oxygen problem and very quickly will be unable to help anyone.

This book has two goals in training you to be a hero. The first is to secure your own mask. The second is to give you the tools you need to get the masks on the people around you.

The first approach will get you thinking about yourself as the hero of your own story, sticking to Definition 1. It will help you deal with your life as it is now and prepare you for the roads to come. It's going to be you-focused.

The second approach is going to focus on how to help those around you. It will help you prepare to be a Reaction Hero from Definition 2. It will give you what you need to improve the world by becoming an Action Hero. It's going to be other-focused.

So, two clearly different uses of the word "hero." But I think you'll see that the first makes the second easier.

∿→ PUT IT ALL TOGETHER! ←∿

So what do we have so far?

- There are two definitions of a hero: the hero in a story, and everyday heroes (which can be Idols, Action Heroes, or Reaction Heroes).

- There are five main steps on every Hero's Journey: the Mundane World, the Call to Adventure, the Threshold, the Path of Trials, and the Master of Two Worlds.

- You don't have to be perfect to be a hero; no one is perfect!

In the next chapter, I'll dive deeper into those five steps, which describe the steps of a fictional character's story. You bought (or borrowed, had gifted, stole, were assigned) this book because it promised to teach you how to be a hero and now it seems like we're back to talking about fictional heroes. Is this a trick? No, let me explain.

CHAPTER 2

WHAT IS YOUR HERO JOURNEY?

Imagine an invisible person is following you around, writing down everything you do and say. In a non-creepy way. This person has a giant book and they're writing a story—your story. You're obviously the main character of this story and, thus, the hero. If every hero story ever written follows the path of the **Hero's Journey**, then it makes sense that yours does too. Right? Right. Let me give you an example.

Depending on where in the world you're reading this, you might have to change some of the details, but most of us have probably had an experience like this.

It's springtime. You're in fifth grade. Elementary school is pretty easy these days. You could find your way around the school in a blindfold. You know the work—there aren't many surprises left. You know who the cool teachers are and who the scary teachers are. It's your normal world: your Mundane World.

Then, like every other hero, you get a Call to Adventure. It's your report card. It tells you that you've passed fifth grade and will be heading to middle school next year. Middle school is like another world. You've heard stories about it—some good, some not so good.

After a lovely, relaxing summer vacation, you find yourself standing at the front door of the middle school. Once you cross that threshold (a literal threshold) you enter a new world. You can't go back to elementary school. No one gets to spend their whole life in elementary school. Well, no one except the teachers.

After stepping through that door, you start on a Path of Trials. There will be new kids, new teachers, and new support staff. Some will become friends, some will be your greatest foes, and many will be the supporting cast of your story. You will face challenges just like every other hero. While you may not get a literal troll, you might encounter trolling in school or online. How you deal with them will change you. You're likely to get lost in the first week. You might forget your locker combination, and who knows what might happen with the food in the cafeteria?

When you come out of middle school as a Master of Two Worlds, you will have changed. So will your school, your family, your community, and the world. How you use the knowledge earned on your journey will define your story.

The Hero's Journey is a cycle. It doesn't actually finish with the Master of Two Worlds. Your new world will become Mundane soon enough and another Call to Adventure will arrive. As you go through school, you'll encounter new challenges like learning to drive, prom, and acne. After that, you'll receive all sorts of Calls. You might go to college, build a business, travel the world, get a job, start a family, or join the circus. All of those things will have their own Thresholds and Paths, and they'll all change you.

CHECK OUT THE SCIENCE!
Self-efficacy

Self-efficacy is belief in yourself and your ability to succeed. It can be what motivates you and helps you achieve your goals … but it can be hard to believe in yourself unconditionally! Especially when you're just starting on your new journey and have a whole path of trials spread before you. But the good news is, there are things you can do to boost your self-efficacy!

Learning new intellectual skills, such as how to plan to reach your goals (we'll talk about that later in this book!), how to best schedule homework and activities, and how to study effectively can really help. And as you become more capable, your self-efficacy will grow—so keep working at those skills you want, even when it's hard. The more you successfully handle challenges, even small ones, the more you will believe you can successfully handle challenges—even big ones! It's all brain training!

You may have already recognized that this means everyone else around you is also on their own hero's journey. That means your classmates, your siblings, your parents, and even that random person watching you read this book. They might be in a Mundane World dreaming of how to escape. They may have just received a Call to Adventure and are wondering if they should accept that call. Perhaps they've just started on the Path of Trials and are finding the journey tough to handle.

So, the point of these early chapters is to get you to think of yourself as the hero of your own story. I want you to see yourself in the spotlight.

> "We have not even to risk the journey alone;
> for the heroes of all time have gone before us."
> —Joseph Campbell, *The Hero With a Thousand Faces*

If you accept that your journey has the same steps as every other hero, then you can use their stories to help you through yours. No one has lived the same story you're living, but everyone has been through the same steps.

This is a powerful tool. If you're going to a new school, consider how Aang handled arriving 100 years in the future. Think about how Mulan left behind everything she knew, or how Frodo stepped outside of the Shire for the very first time. These heroes have advice for us if we're willing to listen. In fact, the only stories that last are those with strong messages that help us in our own journeys. Also, don't forget that it's not just fictional heroes that have been through these steps. While I can guarantee that your grandmother's school experience was different from yours, she can certainly relate to the steps you're going through. Your dad's first week of a new job feels pretty similar to your first week at middle school. You can ask them for advice on how to handle the struggles you feel on your journey.

With that explanation out of the way, let's do a deep dive. I'll be sharing more examples, some stories from my life (scary), and activities to help you best take advantage of this Hero's Journey idea.

THE MUNDANE WORLD

The first time I saw the hero's journey clearly in my life was when I left Australia to work for three months at an American summer camp. I was 21 years old and had been spinning my wheels at university, not putting in the effort I should have been and suffering for it. Then I saw an article in the local newspaper about a guy who had traveled to America to work at a summer camp. That was my Call to Adventure. I accepted that Call and traveled to Michigan. My life changed forever.

The entire time I lived in America, people regularly asked me how I could possibly have decided to move from Australia to Michigan. Australia is a world of dreams for many Americans. It wasn't so dreamy for me. What was mundane for me was not for them.

Many years later, while staying at a vineyard in France on the coast of the Mediterranean, a local woman asked me how I could think her home was so amazing when I'd grown up in Australia. Part of me was still shocked that she didn't think her own home (a vineyard! In France! On the coast of the Mediterranean!) was amazing, but I knew why she asked. I'd asked a version of that question myself 11 years before. In Switzerland.

When I arrived in New York City for my orientation to American life through the camp program, I met Petra on that first night. Like me, Petra had come from a long way away to be a counselor—she had come all the way from Switzerland. I summoned the courage to talk to her and was rewarded with an invitation to stay with her if I ever visited Switzerland. Fast forward two years and she picked me up at the train station. We drove through the Alps to a cafe for lunch. I'd never seen mountains before and here I was having lunch surrounded by them. I said, "You must walk around looking up all the time—it's so beautiful." I was answered with, "Oh, we don't really notice them." Later that week I went out to a cafe and sat with a dozen Swiss locals my age. They had all fled the country at some point to find adventure and to escape the boredom. I asked, "Why would you want to go to Australia when you are living in the middle of Europe in the mountains?" Now I know.

Your Mundane World is yours. It is not a physical place, it's a state of mind.

That's important to realize. The Mundane World is boring, but often only to the hero. Lots of people can agree that growing up on a farm in Kansas or on Tatooine would be boring. That's why the writers of those stories chose those locations. However, I bet you know someone who would trade their left foot for a chance to grow up on a farm. They could work with cool machines, care for animals, and live in the peace and quiet!

A great example of this "how can that be boring?" problem can be found in the book and film, *How to Train Your Dragon*. Hiccup, the main character (hero), starts his story living in a village that regularly fights raiding dragons. That's pretty exciting to me. For him, it was boring. He dreamed of being able to pursue his interest in design and invention. Learning how to fight dragons was mundane—that's what everyone else did. Similarly, T'Challa starts his movie story living in a nation hidden from the world that has technology so advanced that it seems more magic than science. Sounds good to me.

Sometimes when you're talking to someone about wanting to escape your Mundane World, they won't understand. They'll say things like, "Oh, but you have such an amazing family" or "You're so lucky to be able to go to that school" or "Just be thankful for what you already have." You need to remember that it's okay for them to see your world as something different. You're the one living in it—you get to decide if it's boring.

THE CALL TO ADVENTURE

When I received that Call to Adventure in the newspaper, I was ecstatic, but I was also nervous. I recruited a friend into my excitement. We imagined traveling to America and then across to Europe, enjoying adventure after adventure. We shared the same Call to Adventure and went to three or four information and training nights as we prepared for the journey.

But he didn't go to America. He changed his mind at the last minute. He refused the Call.

Refusing the Call is a common occurrence in the hero's journey. The hero says no to the invitation. In Star Wars, Luke Skywalker initially turns down the opportunity to finally leave his planet with Obi Wan and the droids. He has responsibilities. His aunt and uncle need him. He couldn't possibly leave now—maybe later. His words echo those of his uncle from an earlier conversation. Han Solo also initially refuses an opportunity to stay and help the Rebellion. Safety and money are his motivators.

The purpose of the Call to Adventure is to wake the hero up. It shows them that there's something else available outside of the Mundane World. The Call can come in many forms—Frodo's ring, Dorothy's tornado, or Miles Morales' spider. There's often a person involved too; Gandalf helps explain the ring, Glenda welcomes Dorothy to Oz, and Gwen Stacy helps explain the importance of crimefighting.

For us real-life folks, it's opportunity knocking. It might be a new student at school or a chance to take a trip. It could be a new book club starting up or some neighbors moving in. These are signs of an opportunity for change. And for growth.

It is a choice. And like any choice, we can choose not to accept.

But a full refusal of the Call ends the story. You can't be the hero of the story without a story. If Luke had continued to say no to Obi Wan, there would be no Star Wars.

It's a weird thing. We acknowledge that we're living in a Mundane World, and we crave escape. But when an opportunity knocks, we often draw the curtains and pretend we're not home. Why would we spend hours dreaming of adventure only to turn it down?

Fear.

Behind each reason for staying where we are is fear. We might think we're not good enough. We might worry about being embarrassed in front of new people. We might not want to leave the perceived comforts provided by the Mundane World. We may think we just need to "get through it." That's all fear. The greatest enemy of fear is a mirror. Stare down your fears—make them explain themselves. They're unlikely to have answers for you, because there is rarely logic in fear.

Thankfully, we don't always get just one chance. When Simba, the future Lion King, refuses the call from Nala because he's enjoying a "no worries" life, he is given another opportunity when Rafiki shows him the need for accepting the responsibility.

Amelia Earhart said, "When a great adventure is offered, you don't refuse it."

You should always be watching for a Call to Adventure so you can answer it. However, make sure you've made your peace with the Mundane World, because it has ways of making you stay.

CROSSING THE THRESHOLD

It would be easy to consider the scenic drive into my camp as **Crossing the Threshold**. Before that dirt road, I knew nothing of this camp world. When I reached its end, I was in camp. Makes sense. And it could be that easy, but there's a reason I included this step as one of my five important phases when cutting down Joseph Campbell's 40-something steps.

There's a lot of story-based value in creating a definitive threshold for a hero to cross. Who can forget Dorothy stepping out of the black and white world of her Kansas home into the vibrant color of Oz? There's a reason you still hear people talking about taking the red pill 20 years after *The Matrix* came out—it's an iconic piece of Neo's story. Memorable moments make for memorable stories (and money in book sales or movie tickets).

Importantly, the Threshold is often the site of the first test for the hero. This test makes sure the hero is ready for what's to come. Done well, this test can be as iconic as the simple crossing but serves a vital part of the journey.

When Peter Parker is bitten by the radioactive spider and discovers his new powers, his first impulse is to use them for personal gain. Peter is not popular at school. Yes, that's an understatement. He dreams of being able to date Mary Jane but doesn't think she will want to date him. But his spider powers open up a clear route to MJ's heart (or so he thinks). He thinks if only he can get some money to get a car he'll impress her and she'll go out with him. (You'll have to watch the movie to see how well that worked for him.) His mind is on improving his own life. That is not the way of the hero, and Peter gets a terrible wake-up call.

A bitter Peter deliberately lets a robber run past him to prove a point to the wrestling promoter who cheated him out some money. Soon after, that robber kills Peter's uncle, Ben. Ben's lingering lesson to Peter is that with great power comes great responsibility. That is his true threshold. Spider-Man is born in that moment—a hero focusing on the needs of others.

Frodo and Samwise also have a test as they cross the Threshold in the *Fellowship of the Ring*. The simple Threshold crossing is when Sam stops Frodo to point out that with their next step, they will have traveled further than ever before. They're literally leaving the old world behind and embarking on a journey into a strange, new world. However, it is at the Prancing Pony that they're tested to make sure they're ready for that road ahead. Strider meets them there at the behest of Gandalf and does everything he can to make sure they're taking this mission seriously. He says, "Are you frightened? Not nearly frightened enough."

Uncle Ben and Strider serve as **Threshold Guardians** to their respective heroes. Often at the Threshold, a person (or some sort of living thing) stands guard. The Guardian may be an adversary, a neutral bystander, or a potential ally. They may help with advice or try to test the hero's readiness. Their goal may be to stop the hero from entering altogether.

When I arrived at my Michigan camp and crossed the Threshold, I met a few Guardians. Mark and James were the veteran camp staff members who helped explain the laws and lore of this new world. During the week of staff training, they watched over me (and others) to make sure we were ready for the adventures to come. They challenged me, taught me, and warned me.

Your entry into a new school will be guarded. You may bump into another student who is intent on asserting their authority through bullying or posturing. There may be a teacher who throws a surprise quiz at you in the first week.

Your parents are going to be involved in every Threshold crossing for quite a while. They will struggle between wanting you to grow and have new experiences and wanting you to stay exactly as you are, staying safe. How many times have you heard some expression of, "I wish you wouldn't grow up—just stay the way you are"? Parents (I'm one) want you to learn and grow in their heads, but their hearts often cancel that out with a desire to keep you safe. It can help if you remember that any time they seem to be holding you back. They're Threshold Guardians—it's their job to be mysterious and/or test your readiness and/or prevent you from crossing.

The Threshold Guardians, while not always adversaries, have to be dealt with. You need to pay attention to their advice, avoid their diversions, or solve their problem. Above all, acknowledge them.

THE PATH OF TRIALS

The bulk of the hero's story occurs on the Path of Trials. In a movie, the path takes up at least an hour. In a book, three quarters of the chapters are dedicated to it. It is here that the hero meets new people, learns new skills, and overcomes challenges.

Companions

No hero goes on the journey alone. They have companions. This applies to fact and fiction. Percy Jackson is the name in the title, but Percy would be nowhere without Annabeth and Grover. Dorothy has her famous friends on the Yellow Brick Road. Likewise, Martin Luther King, Jr. and Amelia Earhart would not have been able to complete their famous stories without a set of companions and supporters helping them along the way. The same goes for you.

Companions provide complementary skills, knowledge, and perspectives. Frodo's Fellowship of the Ring allowed him to pass obstacles that would have been impossible for him alone. Aragorn, Gimli, and Legolas provided fighting ability and knowledge of the wide world; Samwise provided undying support; and Pippen and Merri gave light-hearted relief. Katniss was aided by the experience of Haymitch, the resourcefulness of Peeta, and the creativity of Cinna. Your choice (yes, it is a choice) of companions can make your journey easier or more difficult.

Mentors

Equally, no hero is without a mentor. Often an older person with the wisdom that age brings, the mentor helps the hero with advice. They're rarely side-by-side with the hero on the path, but they drop in and out of the story with pearls of wisdom. Apart from the white-beard brigade (Gandalf, Obi Wan, Merlin, etc.), you can find Moana's grandmother, the Matrix's Morpheus, and Buffy's Giles. (As an aside, if you're writing a story, maybe it would be a good idea to have a female mentor . . . they're still too few and far between.)

Your mentors are less likely to be wizards than teachers, family members, or coaches. Their advice might not always make sense to you, but take note anyway. It's sure to come in handy later. Ask Po, the Kung Fu Panda, or Remy, the rat chef in Ratatouille.

Villains

Finally, what kind of hero story would we be writing if there wasn't a villain? Dorothy and the Wicked Witch, Luke Skywalker and Darth Vader, Gandalf and Sauron. We match these people up as easily as peanut butter and jelly. While it's rare to have such a dedicated villain in our real-life stories, we certainly encounter adversaries. We're more likely to have a bunch of stormtroopers than a Sith Lord or flying monkeys than a Wicked Witch. Martin Luther King, Jr.'s "villain" was the entire structure of society and the racism that permeated it; not one specific person. In your school life, you'll probably encounter bullies, a teacher who actively dislikes you, or a romantic rival. Or maybe you'll encounter injustices that you want to right.

Skills

Mulan learns "hard" and "soft" skills after leaving home to join the army. Hard skills are measurable. It's things like archery, horse riding, and avoiding sleeping in. Soft skills are definable, but hard to measure. It's things like fitting in with new people, learning when to break school rules for a greater good, and the power of friendship.

The hard skills are often important at key moments during the Path of Trials, but it's the soft skills that create the change in the hero. The soft skills are often learned via the challenges laid out on the path without the hero even noticing they're learning them.

At school, it's easy to see the hard skills you're learning. They're the ones you get tested on. And boy, do you get tested! Tests and tests and tests. There are no (literal) tests for social skills, life lessons, or successful dating. Those are the soft skills and they're the things that change you.

In my summer camp story, I met mentors in James and Mark who taught me how to be respected. I met friends in Crystal, Shannon, and Kim. I met enemies too. That group of people was often part of the skill-learning process. I got first-hand experience in group dynamics and public speaking. I was taught how to connect with children. I even had crash courses in horse riding and car driving—actual crashes included. The challenges were numerous. Some I encountered in public, and some I suffered through in private.

My Path of Trials changed me forever. And that change leads us to the final step—**The Master of Two Worlds**.

THE MASTER OF TWO WORLDS

After my summer at camp, I returned home to Australia. Everyone noticed the transformation. I was confident, happy, and had direction. Before the journey I had been depressed, lonely, and shy.

The final step on the hero's journey is not really a step, just as the first wasn't. This step is a title. At the end of the journey, the hero has changed. It is this change that provides the title of "Master of Two Worlds." The lessons and skills learned in the new world allow for success (and mastery) in the old world. This change in the hero is the whole reason the story exists. Without change, we'd have no interest. Who wants to read 500 pages about a teenager with no super powers who lives with his aunt and uncle and never goes anywhere?

Likewise, at the end of elementary school or middle school (or high school for that matter) you are going to be a different person than the one who started the journey. You will obviously be taller and probably have a different haircut, but most of the change will be on the inside.

> **"Where you arrive does not matter as much as what sort of person you are when you arrive there."**
> —Seneca, *Letters from a Stoic*

ROUND AND ROUND WE GO

You can't be a Master of Two Worlds for long. New worlds start getting normal pretty quickly. Our life ends up being a series of journeys in which we start as inexperienced noobs and work our way up to confident masters.

The Star Wars movies make this concept a major part of the stories. We see Anakin Skywalker as the apprentice of Obi Wan Kenobi and then assume dominance as Darth Vader. We see Luke Skywalker go from farm boy to Jedi Master and mentor to Rey. Obi Wan is also shown in both apprentice and master modes.

The same thing happens in our lives.

My last year of elementary school was a time of great joy. I was king of the playground. I was picked first for cricket matches and never lacked people to hang around with.

It then came as a great surprise when I moved to a new, bigger city to attend a new, bigger school, and found myself at the bottom of the social ladder. No one knew who I was. No one picked me for their sports team. I was distraught.

I sensed what I was in for on the first day of school. I sat in the front seat of the car with my mum, crying my head off. I didn't want to go into this new world. Two older girls walked past the car and asked if they could help. You can imagine how happy I was about that—two girls seeing me crying. They managed to convince me to get out of the car and told me to meet them at lunch time to check in. I went into this new adventure a little more comfortable. But not for long.

For some reason, I was being regularly kicked in the shins during the day as older kids walked past me. Other than that, things were going okay. I told the girls at lunch time. They laughed in the way you would for a new puppy who keeps falling over. They knew exactly why I was being kicked. Our school uniform included knee high light blue socks. According to the school rules, these socks were to be pulled all the way up to the knees. Naturally, I followed the rule. It turned out that no one else did and that the punishment for following that rule was to get kicked in the shins. I rolled my socks down and went on with the business of trying to survive this most stressful of journeys.

This up and down cycle happens in the adult world, too. When I bought my first car, it was from the father of a friend of mine. He was the most senior Volkswagen service manager in the state. He had a great reputation and told me that if I ever had trouble when I was out of town that all I had to do was mention his name at the closest dealership and I would be taken care of. He was clearly at the Master of Two Worlds stage. A few years later, he was let go because the dealership could no longer afford him. I didn't see him for a few years as he bounced around looking for a steady job. One day I went back to the original dealership for a service for my trusty Jetta, and there he was at the front desk. He had taken an entry level mechanic job and was having to learn everything from scratch. He was fighting with the computer because when he worked his way up the ladder the first time, there were no computers. So here was a man who had gone from master to apprentice and you could see how frustrated he was.

It is always tough to start a new journey when you were so comfortable in the last one. This happens all through schooling. You spend years getting closer to the top at your current school and then, bam, you go to a new school and find yourself at the bottom again. However, the fact that you can predict this is a huge bonus. It allows you to prepare. It also allows you to leave a legacy. Most heroes don't get this advantage.

CHECK OUT THE SCIENCE!
Resiliency

Resilience is the ability to bounce back after a challenge, like changes in schools, struggles at home, difficulties accomplishing your goals, or any difficulties in every day life. More resilience helps you do better in school, get along better with others, and be more positive in general.

And building resilience is easier than you might think! One way to do it is just to practice activities and talents you enjoy—plus some of those self-efficacy skills we talked about earlier, like working on attention and problem-solving skills. Healthy, supportive relationships—both with other kids and with adults—also help a lot. Building relationships through common interests and activities (like fun clubs, teams, or community activities) combines all of these strategies.

PUT IT ALL TOGETHER!

Now we know a little more about how Hero Journeys work:

- Hero Journeys are cycles; no one finishes one journey and is set for the rest of their life!

- Everyone's journey and steps are unique to them; there's no right way to do it. Your mundane world is yours, your calls are yours, your trials are yours. You don't have to compare your journey to anyone else's.

- Resiliency and self-efficacy are key to being able to go round and round the hero journeys you'll be on throughout your life.

It all seems pretty straightforward at this point, right? So if being a hero is just going on a journey, going through life, why aren't there more everyday heroes in the world?

CHAPTER 3

WHY AREN'T THERE MORE HEROES?

Have you ever seen something that you knew was wrong, but didn't do anything about it? Yeah, me too. Everyone has experienced it. Instead of taking action, more often than not we do nothing. When I am speaking in front of a large crowd, I often ask people to raise their hand if they think they'd come to help me if I collapsed on the stage. Almost everyone shoots their hand up straight away, saying to themselves (and sometimes to me), "I would definitely help." They say that because everyone wants to think they'd do the right thing. The truth is that nearly all of them (or actually all of them) would stay right where they were. We know this because we see it repeated every time there is a Real Action Hero story in the news. While one person jumps onto the subway tracks, 50 others stand and watch. One person swims out to save the drowning child while twenty others stay on the shore.

THE OPPOSITE OF A HERO

Why don't people help when they know they should? Why don't people help when they said they would? There are lots of reasons. Every one of these reasons exerts a real force on us to remain inactive. When you remembered a time that you chose inaction over action, at least one of these reasons was to blame. Don't feel bad—it isn't that you're a bad person. These hurdles appear for every hero.

This is such an important issue. You can tell by all of the quotes from famous people listed below. They all saw the issue with doing nothing. If you don't believe me, believe them.

> "He who does not prevent a crime when he can, encourages it."—Seneca

> "The hottest places in hell are reserved for those who, in a period of moral crisis, maintain their neutrality."—John F. Kennedy (paraphrasing Dante's *Inferno*)

> "The sad truth is that most evil is done by people who never make up their minds to be either good or evil."—Hannah Arendt

> "In the end, we will remember not the words of our enemies, but the silence of our friends." —Martin Luther King, Jr.

> "Being harassed is terrible; having bystanders pretend they don't notice is infinitely worse."—Celeste Ng

> "We must always take sides. Neutrality helps the oppressor, never the victim. Silence encourages the tormentor, never the tormented."—Ellie Wiesel

> "The world is in greater peril from those who tolerate or encourage evil than from those who actually commit it."—Albert Einstein

> "If you are neutral in situations of injustice, you have chosen the side of the oppressor."—Desmond Tutu

But really, you should believe me—after all, you've read thousands of my words already. Once, when talking to a journalist from a London newspaper, I said the following line:

> "The opposite of a hero is not a villain; it's a bystander."—Matt Langdon

He said, "You should write that down. It's a good one." So, I did. It has become my catchphrase. Upon seeing something wrong, a **bystander** does nothing. A hero does something.

I went to camp with my school in ninth grade. Teachers used to always say teaching the ninth graders was the hardest because everyone was experimenting with who they were. I guess I was no different.

We piled onto buses and drove to a place near the beach. When we stopped, the teachers stood up and explained how we were going to work out where everyone was going to sleep. "Get into groups of eight and go claim a cabin." Now, I am sure you can imagine the scene. Everyone got off the bus and frantically tried to get their groups together. It was pandemonium.

I saw an opportunity in the chaos. I saw my group of friends working on getting an octo-pod together and I also saw a group of the cool kids working on their eight. Now, it's going to surprise you to think I was ever not cool, but it's true. I was not cool in ninth grade. Or tenth or eleventh or twelfth, but those are for other stories.

I thought that if I could get myself into the cabin of cool kids for a week of camp, I'd be set for the rest of my life. After a week, I'd be a cool kid too. It was simple.

After taking a deep breath, I approached the group and asked if I could be in their cabin. Somewhat surprisingly, they said yes. I was in heaven. We headed over to the cabin to drop our stuff off before meeting back at the dining hall. Our circular cabin had four bunks lining the walls. Eight beds. It was at this moment that I realized that the cool kids weren't all that great at math. There were nine of us. I didn't see this as a problem because I would have happily slept on the floor to be in this cabin. I would have slept on a bed of nails had it been presented to me. A mattress was brought in by one of the camp staff and everything was fine.

The rest of the day was spent going through the normal camp things. A tour, an explanation of the rules, dinner, and a night hike. When we got back to the cabin and into bed, it became clear that I'd made a terrible mistake.

A boy in the top bunk started asking me questions. Are you dumb? Why don't you have any friends? Why are you so ugly? It took me by surprise. One of the other guys joined in. A few others laughed along, and the rest just stayed silent. I tried to deflect. I tried to fire back insults. I tried to ignore. None of that worked. In fact, the ignoring tactic spurred him on. He started putting pieces of paper in his mouth, chewing them up, and then spitting them down at me. He got the same reactions from the crowd. One joined, some laughed, some ignored. I failed to get him to stop and ended up slipping deep into my sleeping bag, quietly crying.

We had very little money when I was a kid. My sleeping bag was newly purchased after a long period of saving. It was a point of pride. In the morning, it was covered by hundreds of spitballs, hardened overnight. I don't know what happened after that—I must have been moved to another cabin. I honestly can't remember anything else from the rest of the week of that camp experience.

I'm not telling you this story to make you feel sorry for me. I know it's not an uncommon type of experience and I know many others have plenty worse than that. I wanted to share it to show the different reactions people can have when they see something wrong.

Obviously, there was someone bullying in this situation. But this bully had an **Assistant.** The Assistant joins in and helps the bully. There were also **Reinforcers**—the people who laugh at what's happening, or stand around watching, or tell people what happened the next day. And the day after that and the one after that. Then there are the Bystanders who simply stand by and let the bad thing happen. They might walk past, they might stand in silence. Either way, they stand by.

You have all of these roles available to you when you see something wrong. I am sure you can think of times you've played each of them. The one role that was missing from my story was the Hero. The Hero does something instead of nothing. Imagine if one of those other kids had said something that night. They could have stopped it all. This book aims to help you get ready to be that person, that hero, for someone who needs you.

The opposite of a hero is not a villain; it's a bystander.

We're going to talk about some of the reasons we sometimes remain bystanders—the hurdles to heroism. Don't let it get you down; we'll also talk about how to get over those hurdles.

NOTICE A NEED

It's hard to do the heroic thing if you don't even see the opportunity.

Early in 2012, a young man was waiting for his subway train in New York City. Like most of the people around him, he had his headphones on and was staring at the ground in front of him. He was at the edge of the platform so he could get on the train first. He'd been waiting for a while, so he knew the train had to be pretty close. Then he felt a bump from his left. He looked up to see people crowding around trying to get a glimpse of the tracks. There was a man laying motionless a few feet below him. Our man jumped down right away to lift the victim up off the tracks before the train arrived. In interviews later, he said that he'd been "in his own world" before the bump brought him back to reality.

How often are you "in your own world"? We do it while waiting for a train. We do it when we walk down the halls at school. It's easy to spend hours of your day just looking at your phone. There's nothing wrong with spending time in your own world—that's how I get all of my best ideas. However, you should think about how much time you are spending there

CHECK OUT THE SCIENCE!
Morals and Empathy

Moral development is an important topic, which we'll talk about a few times in this book. Moral values are things that we all commonly define to be right or wrong, like being honest or taking responsibility. Moral values are like rules that guide your behavior.

We start learning about right and wrong as soon as we're born. Even babies can see and mimic the emotions of others, which is a first step to developing **empathy** (the ability to understand what others are feeling and put yourself in their shoes). Empathy is natural and automatic, but it can grow or shrink based on your experiences. Parents, peers, society, and cultures encourage social norms and values, such as respect, that are based on empathy.

and where you're doing it. It's impossible to act heroically if you don't observe the world around you. In this case, it took a literal nudge, a bump, to bring him out of his own world and notice the need. You can't rely on someone nudging you at the critical time.

The second part of noticing a need *is* the need. Sometimes it can be difficult to tell if someone really needs your help or if there is something wrong at all. It's pretty safe to say that a person lying prone on a train track is in need. But what about someone who is being made fun of in the hallway? Is it serious or is just some friends playing? What about if you see a student lying on the ground outside of school? That seems like they obviously need help, but is anyone else acting like it's serious? Is there a crowd standing around doing nothing? It can be hard to be the one who acts to help when no one else is. You're going to look silly if you ask someone to stop teasing and both people tell you there's nothing wrong.

It's also hard to act when you're not sure everyone agrees with you that something is wrong. We all have an internal moral code, but each of us has different warning bells. Is this something "wrong" to you, but not to others? How do you decide to act if you're worried you're just being over-sensitive?

This is tough, and it's just the first of the barriers to action. You can start to see why it's difficult and rare to act heroically.

CONTRADICTING VOICES

Once we have noticed that someone needs our help, we might pause because of conflicting voices in our heads. There's always an internal discussion. "If I do this, what will happen?" "If I don't do this, what will happen?"

I remember going by myself to see a movie during the day. Yes, by myself. Don't judge me—it's actually one of the best solo activities, because you're not supposed to talk anyway. When I came out of the screening, I saw a young staff member with one of those scoop and broom combos. For whatever reason, I thought to myself, "What would she say if I asked her if it was okay to sneak into another movie?" I imagined she'd have an internal conversation with contradicting voices. On the one hand, it's against the rules to sneak into a movie, so obviously she should say no because rules are rules and she might lose her job. On the other hand, she might say yes because it's kind of cool to do something dangerous and she might not want to disappoint me because I was standing right there. There's one example.

CHECK OUT THE SCIENCE!
Prospection

We don't often think much about a moral decision, unless it's the very first time we've ever been in a situation like that. You don't have to think about whether helping your parents carry groceries is the kind thing to do, for example. (You may not really want to do it, but you still know that it's considered kind... make sense?) But we do wonder about future possibilities.

Prospection is when people imagine the future, visualize situations, form arguments and counterarguments, and come up with possible outcomes. Like when you daydream about a conversation with your crush, or think about an argument with your parents—what will you say, what will their reaction be, what will your response be to that reaction, and on and on. Thinking and imagining ahead like this is a huge part of how we think and feel about things and how we choose to act. Imagining your possible behaviors and outcomes is one thing humans do nearly automatically—not just about important moral decisions, but even about everyday, boring situations.

Sometimes following the rules and doing the right thing are not the same thing. This can cause conflicting voices. At school, you're told over and over from when you first start kindergarten that you have to be on time. You probably hear a teacher mention it every day as someone tries to slip into class late. This kind of rule gets stuck in your brain and can become automatic. That's certainly the hope of the rule makers. However, what if you're heading to class one day and you see someone on the ground, clearly hurt? If you stop to help, you'll be late for class. They obviously need help and you'd probably say that, of course, you'd stop to help. But our brains are funny. They like to make automatic decisions as often as possible. They don't want to do too much work. Your brain is likely to say, "You have to be to class on time!" And most people will just follow the brain's order to follow the rules. This goes for the rules that are written down and those that aren't. There are always unwritten rules that everyone at school or at home or in town are following. Are you in danger of just following along at the expense of helping someone?

Another common situation that creates conflict in your head is when you might get embarrassed. What if you try to help and it doesn't work properly? You might get laughed at. Avoiding embarrassment is a huge part of your school life. I know I spent a lot of time trying to avoid it. What if you tell someone to stop making fun of someone else and it turns out they're just good friends and are messing around with each other? The important question is what if they're not and they aren't?

We also convince ourselves not to help because of some perceived danger. It could be a danger to our reputation or a physical danger. It's very important for you to consider any risk involved in your actions, but equally important to decide whether the risk is real. I often suggest to my audiences that standing up to a bully is a heroic thing to do. There's some risk there, but it's often way overestimated. So many people tell me the bully will turn on them, but if you look at real events, you'll see that very rarely happens. Bullies don't get successful based on taking on people who stand up to them. They choose targets who aren't going to say anything. So, make sure you consider any risk, but also make sure you're not overstating it.

CHECK OUT THE SCIENCE!
Automatic Decision Making

These automatic moral decisions are basically the brain running on its "default programming." You have programmed your brain to respond, even if you don't realize it. It's like learning math; when you first learn, it's hard, and you probably used your fingers or objects to see how adding and subtracting worked. But after some practice, you could answer a simple math question without even having to think about it. You "program" your brain by making choices, learning, and acting every day. The things that you do most often become easier for your brain, which is why many habits and tasks become automatic. It saves your brain energy and effort. It's efficient for the brain to make decisions automatically—you just need to make sure you're making choices in line with your moral values, and then those automatic decisions will continue to reflect your values.

PECKING ORDER

For three years, I ran the horse program at my summer camp. I spent a lot of time around horses. A LOT of time. I quickly picked up that horses have their own personalities and their own social order.

In my first summer, there were two horses clearly in charge of the herd. Voyager was the king and Lucy was the queen. When we took hay out to the pasture, the other horses let Lucy and Voyager get the first bite. When it was cold and windy, those two got the comfortable spot in the barn. They had good lives. They were at the top of the pecking order.

At the other end of the pecking order was Pony. Pony was short, old, and unpopular. No, Pony is not another name for me. Poor old Pony got the scraps of hay after every other horse had finished. He dealt with winter storms by standing out in the open, waiting for them to end. Luckily, he was cute, so the kids often loved to take care of him.

In between Pony and the king and queen, the other horses spent their days trying to climb higher up the pecking order and avoiding dropping down it. They'd get into fights, kicking and biting, to try to push up the ladder. They'd change which horses they were hanging out with to try to become more popular. I mean, if Lucy and Voyager liked you, you were in good shape in Horseland. If you became friends with Pony, you were shunned.

Does this sound familiar? I saw a lot of similarities with my school life. The popular kids loved life and got to enjoy advantages day in and day out. At the opposite end, kids sat by themselves, got into trouble, and generally hated coming to school. In between, the rest of us were trying to work out the unwritten social rules, get into fights, pick the right friends, and just survive.

What does the pecking order have to do with being heroic? It can be another barrier. If someone is lower in the pecking order than you, you're less likely to help them when they need it. If they're higher than you, you have an interest in helping. Also, if you're higher than someone doing something wrong, it's easier for you to tell them to stop. If you're lower than them, it becomes exponentially more difficult.

Consider this scenario. A student is walking down the hall, trips, and spills their books everywhere. If this person is low in popularity, what happens? How does that change if they're at the top of the pecking order? The first will probably produce laughs. The second is likely to see a scramble of people trying to help.

What about this? You walk up on someone scratching their name into the bathroom wall. If that person is higher than you in the pecking order, it's much more difficult to tell them to stop than it would be if they were lower than you.

The pecking order absolutely affects our ability to act the way we know we should. Doing the right thing might change our social life in a way that is hard to come back from. Once you're hanging out with Pony it's hard to come back.

SOCIAL GROUPS

When we humans were just getting our start in the big bad world, we stuck together in small groups to increase our chances of survival. A group had more eyes, so we could watch out for danger or find something to eat. A group could share resources like food and water. A group could keep us warm at night. A group could produce children to keep the group existing.

The members of our group were very important to us. We'd do anything for them. Sabertooth tiger attacking one of my group? You'd better believe I'd jump in there to save them. One of the group starving? I'd share my last ear of corn. We knew everyone in our group, so a stranger would be obvious. A stranger would not get my last corn, nor would she get my help against the sabertooth.

As we got better at working out how to do this whole living thing, the groups got bigger. We started creating villages and towns and nations. That natural inclination to help our group stayed with us even when we probably didn't need it much anymore. While we didn't recognize everyone in our group anymore, we could identify them by the way

CHECK OUT THE SCIENCE!
Social Hierarchies

Creating **social hierarchies** has helped groups of social animals (including humans!) to survive for hundreds of thousands of years—knowing who to listen to in a crisis means there's less chance of panic and chaos. But scientists also know that being empathic (having empathy, which we talked about earlier—being able to understand and share feelings of another person) and **altruistic** (being unselfish) helped humans survive and thrive, because it means we look out for each other. People who get along better have a better chance of getting along for a long time!

But social hierarchies can sometimes interfere with empathy and altruism. People who are more empathic tend to want more equal relationships between people and groups, whereas people with less empathy crave more hierarchy or social dominance over others.

So social hierarchy is common, and useful, but can be problematic. People tend to obey people they see as authorities, even if it means going against their moral values—as we saw in Stanley Milgram's experiments, where people would follow the directions of an authority figure, the "experimenter" who asked participants to "electrocute" a stranger for missing questions on an exam. And Zimbardo's Stanford Prison Study demonstrated that otherwise average young adults would behave in abusive and disturbing ways if placed in an authority role, the "prison guard," over other average young adults who were selected to be "prisoners." Heroes tend to have more empathy and responsibility for others, even strangers, which diminishes the likelihood of these problems—but it's hard to break the hold of these social hierarchies!

they looked, how they spoke, and by the things they believed. If I lived in a nation of dark-haired people and I saw a blond woman, my natural reaction would be to be suspicious. If they needed help, I would be unlikely to provide it.

This behavior is encoded into our brain now. We have no reason to need it, but there it is, affecting little decisions every day. We trust people in our perceived groups more than those out of it. We help people in the group more than those out of it. We fear people unlike us. This, of course, happens to a greater or lesser extent in each individual, but it's there in everyone.

When Martin Luther King, Jr., was assassinated, a teacher in an all-white classroom in a mostly-white town in Iowa decided to conduct an experiment with her class of 8-year-olds to help them understand what it was like to be discriminated against. The teacher, Jane Elliott, stated to the class that blue-eyed children were better than those with brown eyes. The blue-eyed students started getting benefits in school: they got more play time, second helpings at lunch, and seats at the front of the class. Brown-eyed students were told that it wasn't their fault—they were just genetically not as smart. The kids with blue eyes started acting superior; they bossed the other kids around, laughed at them when they failed, and other such nastiness. The brown-eyed kids stopped answering questions in class and generally became more timid. The next week, she reversed the exercise and had similar results.

This experiment showed us how powerful social groups are, but it also showed how easily we can be told what groups we belong in. That's scary. Lots of the worst people in history have been successful bad guys because they knew how to make smaller and/or marginalized groups hate each other. It's a lot easier to rule a lot of people if they're broken up into lots of little groups instead of one big one. It continues to happen around the world today.

What are our groups today? Some of them are still very much the same as a hundred thousand years ago. The color of skin, the shape of a nose, the sound of an accent or language, the style of clothes we wear. There are plenty of others now, too. The people in your class. Your school. You're more likely to help someone in your school than in the school across town. We create social groups around our favorite music (and musicians), sports (and teams), TV shows and movies, and video games. Whether you're a "cat person" or a "dog person." You can choose almost any characteristic.

My wife and a couple of friends did an experiment for her psychology class when she was at the University of Michigan. On the day Ohio State University came to play football against the mighty Wolverines, the friends set up a car on the side of the road and pretended it was broken down. One of them stood next to the car, trying to get help. They counted how many times someone stopped to help within an hour. They did the experiment three times. The first time the person asking for help wore a plain grey sweatshirt. They counted seven people offering to help. The second time they wore a blue Michigan sweatshirt with its big yellow M. They lost count of how many people offered to help because there were only two people trying to track them all. They were overwhelmed. The third time they wore an Ohio State shirt. Not a single person stopped to help. In fact, numerous people lowered their windows and heckled.

Social groups are powerful, whether we like it or not. They can decide whether you help someone who needs it. Or not.

CHECK OUT THE SCIENCE!
Expanding Empathy

It's easier to have empathy for people who are like you. But you can be empathetic to just about anyone if you just put yourself in their shoes (meaning imagine what it is like to be them and what they are going through). Pretty simple, right? Another way is to practice **loving-kindness meditation,** where you intentionally focus on loving your own self and gradually expand your attention to people close to you and eventually further away, to include all of humanity. It's like visualizing yourself pushing out loving and kind feelings toward others. These "training" methods are really simple ... you just need to actually take some time to do them!

THE CROWD

Would you jump off a bridge if everyone else was doing it?

It's a popular question from parents around the world. The problem is that, in practice, the answer is often yes. Humans are very good at being sheep. Sheep follow the masses, stay in the group, agree with the group. Of course we're going to jump off the bridge. If everyone else is doing it, there must be a good reason. Right?

The real reason your parents are asking the question is the hope that you'll make a smart and safe decision instead of blindly following others. Our brains are great at creating short cuts and following patterns. If a big group of people are doing something, then our brain makes the assumption that it must be fine.

In 1951, a psychologist named Solomon Asch decided to test his observation that people seemed to do whatever everyone else was doing, regardless of whether it was right or not. He created a set of 18 slides that had a thin black line on the left and three on the right. One of the lines on the right was the same length as the one on the left. The other two were obviously of different lengths.

Asch presented the slides to groups of eight people, asking them to identify the line on the right that had the same length as the line on the left. Sounds pretty simple, right? He purposely made the length of the lines very different, so it should be easy to tell; when giving the test individually, less than one percent of people got the answer wrong.

Then the real test began. Instead of testing people individually, he tested eight people in the same room together. The eight participants sat around a table and, one by one, went around answering the question. Except seven of the eight people weren't real participants at all—they were actors! Occasionally, when signaled by Asch, all seven actors gave the wrong answer, and the sole real participant watched them do it. When it came time for the real participant to give their answer, suddenly the test wasn't so straightforward.

Asch tested 50 people. Seventy-five percent of the real participants gave at least one wrong answer, swayed by the crowd. Only twenty-five percent of people were confident enough to give the correct and obvious answer. Five percent gave the wrong answer every single time, conforming to the group.

Now, these people weren't jumping off a bridge, but they were giving the wrong answer to a very simple question. If

CHECK OUT THE SCIENCE!
Peer Pressure

People tend to hang out with other people who are similar to them. No surprise there. And over time these groups become even more similar to each other! You might become friends with some people because of a similar taste in music; you all talk and hang out and compare music, and eventually you don't just listen to similar music, you're all listening to the same few bands.

Group relationships are an important part of figuring out your own identity, and going along with the group isn't necessarily bad. The infamous "peer pressure" comes about because social groups have norms or "rules" about how members should behave, which affect us even when we're not with the group. Most people talk about the negative parts of peer pressure that we all know, like bullying, substance abuse, school drop-out rates, or risky behavior.

These are all real concerns, but there's also plenty of positive peer pressure! People encourage each other to volunteer, give back, and generally work to make their communities a better place. Maybe we just need to change the way we think about peer pressure.

so many people will get an obvious question wrong, imagine what it's like when a crowd is doing something that you're not even sure is the wrong thing.

If everyone in your camp cabin is making fun of the kid on the floor, it's easy to see why you wouldn't do something about it. If no one is doing anything to help the kid who seems to be drowning, then it's easy to assume there's no reason to do anything.

This behavior has been shown in other experiments too. When people were placed in a waiting room and saw smoke coming from under a door, they tended to follow the cues of the other people (who were part of the experiment) in the room. If they were alone, they were much more likely to leave the room and tell someone there was a fire. If no one did anything about it, the test person often didn't either. On the old show, *Candid Camera*, the experimenters were able to get individuals to face the back of the elevator just by having the other people (actors from the show) already in there doing it. YouTube can lead you down a rabbit hole of these sorts of experiments.

If we're so easily influenced by strangers, as seen in the experiments we just discussed, it's clear that our friends exert even more power over our actions. If your friends all love Ariadne Grande but you thought "My Everything" was super bland, it's hard to admit that. If all of your friends are smoking and gambling on Friday nights, it's pretty hard to do otherwise. If your friends all pick on a certain person in class, it's hard to say anything.

NORMS

We often too easily follow what the crowd or what our group thinks, but we're not actually very good at knowing what they think in the first place. We spend a lot of time behaving in the ways that we think the pecking order prefers, the group expects, and the crowd wants. These things are called norms. Or **social norms,** if you want to be picky. They're the things that are normal in our group. That group could be your school, your country, your age group—any of the possibilities we discussed before. All of the hundreds of thousands of different groups have different norms.

CHECK OUT THE SCIENCE!
Asch's Experiment

This study was looking at conformity—whether people would behave independently from how a group behaved or if they would follow the group. When people talk about this experiment, they always talk about how many people conformed. But some people resisted the social pressure and answered the questions correctly—and those people, who didn't conform in the beginning, didn't break down and conform later. It's also interesting that most people who conformed assumed something was wrong with **them**. They said things like:

"I thought that maybe because I wore glasses there was some defect."

"At first I thought I had the wrong instructions, then that something was wrong with my eyes and my head."

"Maybe something's the matter with me, either mentally or physically."

"I felt they must be right and I must be wrong."

When I started working at my camp, the kids (and counselors) around me had very different ideas on which words and phrases were "swear words." In Australia I said "damn" without anyone raising an eyebrow. At camp, eyes would shoot at me like I'd just admitted I liked pineapple on my pizza (I do). The very same word had very different reactions in front of different groups. In many countries in Europe, nakedness on a beach is perfectly normal. Not so at beaches in Michigan. (I'm not speaking from personal experience, by the way.)

Norms tell us how to behave. They're a shortcut, and that's mostly helpful. It's particularly helpful when you find yourself in a new place or group. If we turn up in a new country and everyone shakes hands when they meet, we shake hands when we meet someone. If, instead, they kiss each other on the cheek three times, we kiss them on the cheek three times. If no one in a new group swears, we don't swear. If everyone smokes, we smoke.

The problem comes when we actually think the norm is something it isn't. If we think most people prefer Marvel to DC, we're likely feel pressure to read Marvel. If everyone in our group is drinking Coke and making jokes about Pepsi, we're likely to join the Coke clan. If we sense that most people think bullying is a normal part of life, we're unlikely to challenge it.

But what if those things aren't true?

How would that happen, you ask? Perhaps the Marvel readers are the loudest in your group. Maybe the people who prefer Pepsi don't care enough to get into a fight about it. Maybe no one in your new school ever speaks up against racist jokes. We learn social norms by watching the actions of others. If people are scared to act on what they believe, then anyone observing could easily guess they believe the opposite. You can see how this becomes a vicious cycle.

It is very common for the majority to believe they're in the minority and the minority to think they're the majority. As such, negative behavior can easily take over a group.

MOVING RESPONSIBILITY

It's not my fault. It's not my job. It's not my responsibility.

In 1971, Kitty Genovese was walking home to her apartment in New York City late at night. She was attacked by a man with a knife and screamed out for help. But nobody came. Thirty-eight people allegedly heard her screams, but none of them decided to help. They remained bystanders. I use the word "allegedly" deliberately, because the story has developed a lot of holes in recent years (you can Google it for more information).

But whatever the truth, this story sparked a huge interest in studying why people are more likely to watch than to help. Researchers from the world of psychology started conducting all sorts of studies and came up with the same crazy answer. It seemed that the larger a crowd was, the less likely anyone was to help. They called it the **Bystander Effect.**

We are very good at moving responsibility. It takes me less than a second to see a pile of laundry on the floor and decide someone else should take care of it. The same goes for a pile of dishes. Unfortunately, the same thing happens when we see bigger problems than household chores. When someone needs help or something is wrong, we can just as easily and quickly move the responsibility onto someone else. There are three main ways we do it.

First, we can move it to someone else in the group. Maybe that person is closer. That guy over there is stronger, I'm sure he'll help. If I wait a few seconds, I'm sure someone else will do it. This is the classic Bystander Effect. There are so many people present that it makes sense that someone else will do it. The problem, of course, is that if everyone thinks that way, no one takes action. Remember Wesley Autrey's train track rescue from earlier in the book?

Second, we can assume it is someone else's job. If you see a teacher or a police officer or someone older than you, it's easy to assume they'll do the right thing. After all, that's their job, right? It makes sense that the people whose job is to keep people safe would do so.

CHECK OUT THE SCIENCE!
Bystander Effect

The bystander effect is one of the oldest topics of research in social psychology. Some of the first scientists to study it found that a person by themselves seeing an emergency was likely to help about 75% of the time—but when even just one other bystander was around, the first person helped only about 50% of the time. This has been tested with different ages, ethnicities, genders, and social statuses and the same thing happens: the more and more people are around, the less likely a person is to help. The basic reason for this is that individuals spread the responsibility to everyone there. Someone else has probably already called 9-1-1, I don't need to. Someone else will help. If no one else is helping, the person must not need help. But new research has found that people are more likely to help when a situation is dangerous—which is good news for the likelihood of heroism.

In 1991, Moss Hills was playing piano as part of the entertainment on board the cruise ship, *Oceanos*. One night the seas were so rough that glasses, bottles, and eventually furniture started sliding all over the place. Moss eventually noticed that there was a serious problem with the way the ship was moving and wondered why an evacuation hadn't been declared. A couple of passengers noticed water in the hallways and went to the bridge to ask the captain what was happening. They found that the entire crew had abandoned ship, including the captain! Moss Hills took control, radioing for help, and then supervising the evacuation as 16 helicopters helped rescue the 571 people still on the ship. That's right: the ship's pianist led the rescue in which every single person was saved. The ship sank and the captain was found guilty of negligence. People don't always do their jobs, especially when there's a crisis. You can also check out what happened with the *Costa Concordia* cruise ship in 2012.

Third, we like to blame the victim. That sounds weird— another one of those, "I would never do that" kind of things. It is certainly hard to imagine thinking someone who had fallen onto the subway tracks deserved it. But what if he was on his phone and wasn't paying attention when he fell? It's hard to imagine a woman walking down the street deserving to be attacked. But what if she was walking alone at night? What if the person having a heart attack is obese? Once again, our brains are often not very logical. They can force us to act based on snap judgments. These judgments aren't fair, but they still happen far too often.

The victim-blaming happens a lot in bullying, too. We tell them not to dress like that or talk that way. We say stop hanging out alone or hang out with her, but not him. We advise them to like these things, but not those things. We suggest they should change. We suggest they deserve to be bullied. Now, no one would ever say that directly (well, no nice people anyway), but our suggestions for them to change communicate that very message. As do our actions.

⋀⋀⋏⟶ PUT IT ALL TOGETHER! ⟵⋀⋏⋀

Being a hero is more than just going on a journey! It means paying attention to the world and the people around you. Remember:

- The opposite of a hero isn't a villain; it's a bystander.

- You need to notice a need to do anything about it.

- Our social hierarchies, social norms, and automatic decision-making affect us and our choices more than we think. Practicing empathy and prospection can help you break out of this.

Alright, that's simple enough. Notice a need, be empathetic, and act according to your values. But are we expected to do all this alone? Of course not!

CHAPTER 4

WHO ARE YOUR PEOPLE?

King Arthur's Mundane World saw him living as a poor squire with no prospects. One day he came upon a gathering of people all trying to pull a magical sword out of a rock. It was prophesied that whoever was able to pull the sword out would become king of all of England. This was a big deal as there had never actually been someone who ruled over all of England—the country was made up of many smaller kingdoms all battling for supremacy.

With a prize like that, everyone and their brother (girls were apparently uninvited—silly medieval times) was out trying to pull the sword from its rocky scabbard. Arthur watched as his adopted father and brother gave it a try and then, for some reason, he was encouraged to give it a go himself. Lo and behold, the sword came right out in Arthur's hands. And bam—he was king.

The problem with becoming king before you start shaving is that you have a distinct lack of experience in that particular skill set. Arthur was a good kid, but hardly king material. His

Call to Adventure had put him squarely into an uncomfortable Crossing the Threshold with a pretty stormy Path of Trials in sight. Luckily, Arthur seemed to understand what Joseph Campbell wanted us to understand—you're not alone, because you can learn from all of the other journeys out there.

Arthur ordered a circular table from his magical friend, Merlin, and promptly filled it with people who could give him good advice. King Arthur's **Round Table** was born. Arthur was happy:

> **"And these knights with the Round Table please me more than right great riches."**
> —King Arthur, Malory's *Le Morte d'Arthur*

Sitting around that early table were people with varying backgrounds and proficiencies. Merlin the wizard had wisdom in spades. Sir Kay, Arthur's foster brother, provided the support only a brother could. King Pellinore was able to share his regal experience. Palamedes, the Saracen, provided the perspective of an outsider. Last, but not least, Guinevere offered her insight and education.

Compare this with the modern young entrepreneur who builds an advisory board consisting of people with experience in accounting, law, marketing, and sales. Compare it with Tim Hunter's Trenchcoat Brigade or Percy Jackson's Camp Half-Blood staff.

The inexperienced hero needs guidance from those who have gone before. As we encounter struggles on our journeys, we only need to look to our guides and mentors for help. To assist with this, I propose that we all create our own Round Tables. Now, I don't mean I want you to set up a circular

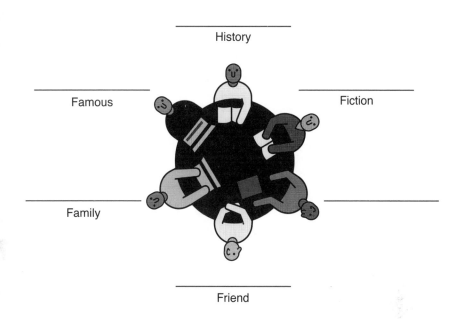

History

Famous

Fiction

Family

Friend

table in your bedroom and have people sit there all day waiting for your questions. That would be creepy. And probably illegal.

I want you to create a metaphorical round table. This table will have seats reserved for the best of the best. The people who sit at your table are chosen for their ability to advise and guide you. Just you. There will be no table exactly like it in the world. Because it is metaphorical, you can have anyone sitting there. They could be people you know or people you've only heard of. They could be real or fictional. They could be living or dead.

You can use the round table on the next page, draw your own on a piece of paper, or print one from apa.org/pubs/magination/hero-handbook.

You will see there are six seats at this particular table. Feel free to add more if you like, but for our purposes here, six is a good start. Each seat also has a label that indicates what kind of person can sit there, so let me explain those to you.

Fiction

This seat is for someone from fiction. That means you could choose from books, movies, TV shows, video games, or comics.

I chose Indiana Jones for this one because I know he would encourage me to take risks and do what's right.

History

Choose someone from history for this seat. It could be someone you learned about in history class, or it could be a deceased relative. It could even be someone you read about in a TIL on reddit.

In this seat, I placed Irene Morgan, who refused to give up her seat on a bus to a white couple eleven years before Rosa Parks famously did something similar. Her tenacity and knowledge of her rights is something I aspire to.

Famous

I've already talked about the difference between a celebrity and a hero, but just because you're famous, it doesn't mean you can't be a hero—or someone's adviser. Use this seat for someone that nearly everyone knows about.

I put Angelina Jolie here because she shows through her actions that she values caring for others and she'd make sure I keep that in mind.

Family

This treasured seat is for someone from your family. You can define this however you like. Choose the person who would give you the best advice on your journey.

This is a bit clichéd, but I chose my mum for this one. She's incredibly practical and I need that.

Friend

This is not a popularity contest, so don't choose your "best" friend just because they'll be hurt if you don't. Choose the friend who is best able to give you good advice.

I chose my friend Chris for this seat. He has a knack for making the right decisions for himself and those he loves even when it means standing up to pressure from those around him.

Blank

This is the spare seat. Use it to place someone who could have been at one of the other seats, but came in second place.

There was a lot of competition for this seat, but I ended up with Shada Nasser. Her fight for human rights, in particular for child brides, was so long and so difficult that she reminds me to never give up.

You can easily come up with other categories if you want to expand this table. In the past, I have used "**Words**" for someone whose words inspired me, "**Actions**" for someone who did things that showed me their value, and "**Story**" for someone whose story made me think they'd make a great advisor.

Naturally, feel free to ignore all the suggestions I just gave and create your own table the way you want to. I did it this way to help get you started. Hopefully the guidelines helped you find seats for some people you might not have thought of without them.

When your table is finished, put it somewhere safe. You could keep it in your locker or a folder at school. You could place it on your bedside table or on your mirror. The point of the table is that you use it. When you're struggling with something on your hero's journey, ask these people for help. (Probably don't actually use your voice to ask them—people might worry about you.) Imagine sitting at the table and asking them questions. Imagine their responses. You know these people well, so it's not hard to guess what they'd say. When I am having a tough time, I often imagine myself sitting at this table. Chris is always fighting to sit next to Angelina. Indiana and my mum have arguments about what's safe for me. Irene just shakes her head at all the fuss. We're a weird bunch, but I always come away feeling better about my situation.

Ready to take it to the next level? Why not create a Round Table of real people to help advise you in real life? I mentioned above that a lot of startup founders create an advisory board with people from different backgrounds and with different skill sets. You can do the same.

Think about the areas you need help with and start recruiting. If you're aiming to be an app developer, you might need some help on the promotional side. If you see yourself killing it on Broadway, maybe you need someone who's been there. Think about your goals and then look at where you're going to need help. Once you've got that list, you need to find people.

You can call on the family member you put on your metaphorical round table. Perhaps there's an artist, or a business person, or firefighter in town that you could add. Maybe you admire someone online. Once you've created a shortlist of people, you need to invite them. This can be done in many ways, but I always suggest going big. Create an official invitation. Make it look great. Explain the concept and what you hope to gain from this person. You could lay out exactly how you plan to utilize this awesome group of advisors. Maybe you'd like to be able to ask them questions whenever they come up. You might want to be able to check in with them once a month or twice a year. How will you contact them? Email, phone, Skype, Twitter? The more information you give your prospective Round Table member, the better your chances of success. You're almost certainly going to get rejections. You'll get non-responses too. Just move on to the next person. If that architect in Chicago didn't respond, send an invitation to the one in San Francisco.

Say you want to find an architect to mentor you, since you're really into eco-inspired houses. You read online that there are a lot of these architects in San Francisco, so you decide to look there first.

1. Google phrases like "eco architect San Francisco" or "eco homes San Francisco." Say you find an article with pictures of cool eco-homes in San Francisco.

2. Then, look for the name of the architect or architecture firm that designed the eco-homes you like. Once you have a name, look for a contact page on their website.

3. Write the email.

    • The Subject Line is important – how can you write it in a way that gets the email opened? There are hundreds of articles about this online, so read a few to figure out your best option.

    • Explain how you found them. "I saw the article on the InHabitat website and loved what you said."

    • Describe the Round Table concept in your own words and why you like it.

    • "I'd like to officially invite you to take one of the six seats on my Round Table." It's nice to show that this invitation is limited—more exclusive.

    • List your expectations. "I plan to email my Round Table every six months to give an update on my progress and ask questions. I may ask you architecture specific questions more often if they come up. You can leave the table at any time, of course!"

4. Press send!

You can use these same steps to contact basically anyone. You can use email, real mail, Twitter, Facebook, or walk into their office if they're local. Most people are thrilled when someone who really wants help asks for it.

You could (and should) create an end of year report for this Round Table too. Each year, write up everything that you've done to move toward your goal. They will want to know the successes and failures. They will also want to know your plans for the coming year. I guarantee that none of them will be expecting it. It will blow them away. And they will never want to give up their seat.

On that point, these Round Tables should not be static. Just because you picked someone today, that doesn't mean they're right for you for the rest of your life. You should feel free to change them up whenever you think someone hasn't got anything to offer you any more or when you meet (or learn about) someone new who looks perfect for your table. Change is good.

THE HERO TEAM

When we see photos of Gandhi, he is usually alone with his poverty. Junko Tabei is alone on the peak of a mountain. Abraham Lincoln is alone behind his podium. Rosa Parks is alone on her bus seat, standing up (or sitting down) for freedom. The hero walks alone.

Except, of course, that's simply not true. It's obvious in fiction, but for some reason the truth eludes us when the hero is an actual living being (or no longer living, as the case may be). Dorothy has her friends closely accompanying her on the Yellow Brick Road. Luke Skywalker also keeps his friends close all the way through his story. Mulan has Mushu, Cri Kee, and Li Shang to help her reach her potential (though Li Shang acts as a threshold guardian for a bit, too). Frodo has the famous Fellowship for the first part of his story, and Sam for the rest.

The set of allies and mentors is a well-known feature of the hero's journey. Simply put, no hero succeeds in their story without the help of other people. No doubt, many of you will take this as a challenge to prove me wrong. Just use hashtag #MattIsAlwaysWrong and I'll be sure to respond.

As with fictional heroes who are the main characters of their stories, you are the main character of your own story. You need help from a community of people just as much as they do. As did Gandhi, Tabei, and Parks. They were each on a hero's journey and had supporters, mentors, advisors, and followers. All of these types of companions are out there for you too. You just need to look.

Most people don't look, so most people get what they're given. It's easy to collect a supporting cast while you're on autopilot. There's the set of people from school just because you happen to be in the same place as them 40 hours a week. There are the friends of friends or the kids of your parents' friends. They just sort of accumulate without you paying any attention. Like socks.

The companions in this sort of autopilot story are random. As with any random collection, there's a wide range. There will be incredibly supportive friends as well as soul vampires and mopers. In between them is a large set of "can't be bothered" until they need something. If this is how you've set up your hero's journey companions, you've probably already thought of some names for each of the types I described.

It's time to choose.

Choose your companions. Start looking for people to fill the roles you need. And start firing those who are holding you back. Your goal is to create a **Hero Team** whose purpose is to support you—to help you create a story worth telling.

While the Round Table included fictional characters and celebrities, or real people you talk to only occasionally, the Hero Team is made up of people who you talk to on a regular basis. Once the team is assembled, direct your energy toward them. That energy will be better spent with them than on the ranks of randoms.

Entrepreneur and motivational speaker Jim Rohn said that we're the average of the five people we spend the most time with. Apart from that being mathematically impossible, he makes a great point. If you spend your time with ambitious people, you're going to become more ambitious. If you spend your time with people who sit on the couch all day, you're likely to have a strong relationship with your own couch. If your five people all want to start their own business before they're 15, you are probably on that path too. If they all play PlayStation instead of Xbox, guess which system you're likely to prefer? Think about those five people and whether they're helping or hindering. Choose your friends. Fire your friends. You have my permission. Every year, I make a list of the people who have made me feel the best and a list of those who made me feel the worst. I then deliberately alter how much time I spend with them. Don't be afraid to stop hanging out with people who bring you down. This isn't about being a cutthroat executive who is looking to profit from everyone, just make sure you're being deliberate about who you're spending time with.

Your team is the key to your success. They are the key to your happiness. Get out there and recruit. Look outside of the everyday places like school or your social circle. Wherever you live there's a community around you full of people you've never met. No doubt, there are dozens of ways to remedy that. As you start meeting these new people, consider what roles they might fill. Interview them. No need for a résumé, but you should be deciding whether you want to invite them to be part of your Hero Team.

Remember that you can also fire people if they're not the kind of team you want. Joe Gatto from "Impractical Jokers" told me that he spent a year at school with no friends for that very reason. He just stopped hanging out with them because they were bad influences. It was a tough year of loneliness and missing out on social events, but he came out of it with a supportive team, three of whom he now spends his days with making people laugh. It's not easy, but it is an option.

One of the positions on your team is perhaps the most important. The mentor is a central figure in most hero stories. There's a reason that Gandalf, Glenda, and Obi-wan are famous characters. They're often the difference between success and failure for the hero. It makes sense that you should have one.

Mihaly Csikszentmihalyi, the author of *Flow*, interviewed nearly a hundred of the world's most creative people and found that nearly all of them had a mentor before they'd finished high school. Mentors are important because they can make suggestions that you've never thought of. This could be in the form of career advice or contacts, but more importantly for hero training, they can introduce you to heroes for your collection and give examples from their own lives on how certain values or behaviors helped or hindered them on their journeys.

Mentors can also offer support in ways that your family and friends can't. They're removed from the politics of those two groups. How often have you chosen not to ask a family member for advice on a tricky situation because you know it would spread through the whole family in about six seconds flat or result in shame or guilt? How about your friend group?

That can be even scarier. Mentors have chosen you. You can be you with them: no faking, no balancing, no guilt.

It's pretty intimidating to find a mentor. Most people aren't lucky enough to have a mentor find them, so how do you go about getting one (or more than one)? If you created that Round Table of real people, that's a good start. A mentor is going to be a more frequent communicator and direct helper than your Round Table members, but maybe one of them could take that step.

The first rule is don't ask them to mentor you. Just like you wouldn't ask someone you like to start dating you in the first conversation; you need to let it happen naturally. Start by asking a specific question that you'd like answered.

That leads to the second rule. Make your question short and make it something you couldn't find out yourself with Google and 20 seconds. You want the potential mentor to feel useful and you want them to notice that you've already put in some effort before coming to them. Consider the difference between asking "Which are the top universities that I should consider if I want to become a film maker?" and "I saw you went to NYU for film school, would you choose it again?"

And finally, the third rule is to show why the two of you make a good match. Are you interested in their field? Have they done things that you admire? Do they show a character trait that you want to know more about? Let them know where you're coming from so they can figure out why they should take you on.

As with any Hero Team member, you should regularly judge whether they're helping you move forward. If they stop responding or start being mean-spirited, or even just change into some other role, feel free to replace them. Mentors are important, but they're not more important than you. Be careful that you don't just blindly do anything they say.

WHAT IS YOUR ROLE?

This chapter has been all about the *other* people on your Hero's Journey. Around your Round Table sit a number of guides, idols, and mentors. Your Hero Team is made up of people who support you day-to-day. Considering all of these people and their roles in your journey is an important piece in the overall puzzle. William Shakespeare is going to introduce the next activity.

> "All the world's a stage,
> And all the men and women merely players:
> They have their exits and their entrances;
> And one man in his time plays many parts."
> —William Shakespeare, *As You Like It*

Teams have all sorts of roles and you're likely to have a unique set on your journey. Here are some examples to get started.

The Cheerleader: The person who is always supportive and positive.

The Action Hero: The person who you can always rely on to get the job done.

The Inspiration: The person who is able to keep you focused on self-improvement.

The Mentor: The person who provides advice and guidance based upon their own experiences.

I can also think of people who fill roles like **The Realist, The Inseparable Friend, The Coach,** and **The Friendly Rival**. Make a chart, and fill out the names of the people who fill all of the roles for you.

I want you to take a 180-degree turn. If all of these people are playing parts in your story, it makes sense that you are playing a role in theirs. Everyone is the hero of their own story, so everyone is on a hero's journey full of characters that help and hinder. You are one of those characters for everyone around you.

As you make your way through your own journey, maybe you're playing the role of mentor to one person while acting as a supportive friend to another. You might even be the villain in someone's story too. Mentors come in all sorts of shapes and sizes, as do supportive friends. One friend might have a great shoulder to cry on (perhaps two), while another might be the cheerleader for all your crazy ideas.

I want you to write down three names. The first is another student at your school (doesn't have to be a friend), the second is a staff member at school (doesn't have to be a teacher), and the third is someone in your family (doesn't have to be immediate family). Now describe the specific role you play in the journeys of each of those three people. I'll start with some examples from my life.

> **Student.** Bertha. I was the funny guy who always made her laugh even when she was feeling low.

> **School Staff.** Mr. Diamond. I made his life difficult by cracking jokes when he was trying to teach us science.

> **Family.** Mom. I helped her out with carrying the groceries, but most of the time I should have helped her more.

Finished yours? Good. Now, consider that every one of those roles is a choice. Your choice. You've chosen to be the friend who checks in every week. It was you who decided to crack that joke. You are the only person involved in the decision to help with groceries.

Every one of these choices can be changed. You may be a bit part in the story of a kid at school, but you could actively increase your role for better or worse. Perhaps you're the thorn in the side of one of your teachers. Why have you made that choice?

Pick someone you know, consider your role, and then think of how you could change it. After all, it's your choice.

Often, the role we think we're playing is not the one that we're actually playing. Take time to really consider the effect you're having on the people around you. Observe your actual actions, rather than your general opinion. You could even ask someone else for their thoughts (though be prepared for the fact that you're probably not going to get a completely objective opinion when you ask someone what they think of you). Seeing yourself through someone else's eyes can be an eye-opening experience.

COLLECT HEROES

> "You are lucky in life if you have the right heroes.
> I advise all of you, to the extent you can,
> to pick out a few heros."—Warren Buffett

So do I, Warren, so do I. In fact, I suggest collecting heroes like you might Pokémon cards or Funko Pops. Heroes are less expensive too, so you have no excuse.

Even heroes have heroes, so that might be a clue as to how useful this practice is. Nelson Mandela, Albert Einstein, Martin Luther King Jr., Cesar Chavez, Barack Obama, the Dalai Lama, and John Lennon all listed Gandhi as one of their heroes. Each one of them was a hero (of the Idol variety) to many others.

Fictional heroes are good to collect too. We've been celebrating hero stories for thousands of years and there's no reason to stop now. They give us direction on how to be better humans, but they can also have immediate effects on our behavior. Psychology professor Lisa Libby was part of a team at Ohio State University that tested those effects. She found that people who got lost in stories of heroes were more likely to act similarly to those very heroes. If the hero in your favorite story overcomes obstacles, then you're more likely to persevere through challenges in your life.

After surviving the mass shooting at Marjory Stoneman Douglas High School in Parkland, Florida, Anna Crean told the website "The Cut" that she knew she and her friends could "make a difference because that's what books and movies have told us since we were little." She and her friends had grown up fighting for justice alongside Katniss in Panem. It was second nature to decide to take action when something horrible happened to them.

I talked about Wesley Autrey in an earlier chapter. He risked his life to rescue someone who had fallen onto a New York City subway track by lying down between the rails. His story was spread around the world and particularly in New York where he was known as the Subway Hero. Chad Lindsey had seen the Wesley Autrey story many times. As a Michigander living in New York, Chad was still enthralled by the subway system, so stories of heroism in that location really hit the mark. One day, that interest became mortally important.

Chad was waiting for his train when he saw a man stumble and fall on to the tracks. As usual, the crowd who also saw it stood frozen. They were affected by any number of the factors we explored in Part 2 of this book—moving responsibility, the crowd, contradicting voices. Chad, however, rushed over and jumped onto the tracks. The man was unconscious, so Chad tried to lift him to the platform. It was not easy—the man was limp and heavy (like when a kid who doesn't want to be picked up goes "boneless"). The crowd watched on. Then Chad heard the train coming. His mind went back to Wesley Autrey. He thought about lying between the tracks and letting the train run over him and the man. Then he snapped out of it and said to himself, "There is NO WAY I am doing that!" He asked the onlookers for help. They helped. The man (and Chad) was saved from certain death. Would Chad have jumped down if he hadn't collected Wesley Autrey's hero story? He doesn't think so.

You can find example heroes in many places. There are plenty of books listing heroes as well as websites dedicated to collecting them. One great place to visit if you have the chance is the Lowell Milken Center in Kansas. They have displays and stories of unsung heroes from around the world created by school students. Their mission is to help kids discover heroes, research them, and then share their stories with the world. The British politician, Benjamin Disraeli, said that the legacy of heroes is the memory of a great name and the inspiration of a great example in a speech to the House of Commons in 1894. The Lowell Milken Center helps remember those names and provides wonderful examples for all of us. There are so many books with collections of heroes that you can find in the library or bookstore.

So, what will your hero collection look like? It could be a set of books on the shelf, a series of portraits that you paint, a notebook with scribble stories that you pick up in your travels, or something else. Start it today and, if you want, share your collection with others. You never know who you might discover when they share back with you.

∿⟶ PUT IT ALL TOGETHER! ⟵∿

No one goes the journey alone! You'll have lots of different people, in lots of different journeys, throughout your life. Some you'll know in real life, some you won't. Some will stick around for a long time, others may not. That's okay! Remember, you're in charge of who's with you on your journeys.

- Your Hero Round Table is a tool to get advice from a variety of people (real or fictional) with a variety of perspectives. Everyone has something unique to offer.

- Your Hero Team is your group of companions. These are the real-life people you interact with regularly. Surround yourself with people who will support you, not drag you down.

- Think about what role you play in other people's journeys; try to be someone who supports other people on their journeys, too.

So what's the point of these journeys? Where are you going? Let's talk about setting some goals.

CHAPTER 5

WHAT ARE YOUR GOALS?

> "If a man does not know to what port he is steering, no wind is favorable to him."—Seneca

PICK A DESTINATION

I imagine Seneca believed the same applied to women. Let's hope. He does make a good point. It's hard to have a successful journey if you don't know where you're headed. A friend of mine, Caspar Craven, told me that unless people know how they can help you, they won't be able to. His advice lines right up with Seneca's. If I don't know you want to be a professional speaker, then I won't be able to share the advice I've accumulated over the years. If I don't know that you're desperate to travel to Budapest, I won't be able to introduce you to my friends who would love to welcome you there.

Having a destination is important for making decisions about opportunities that arise in your life. However, getting to the destination doesn't have to be done in a straight line. In fact, it rarely is. We get to the end via curves, dips, climbs, sudden drops, and river crossings. Author Neil Gaiman imagined his goal as a mountain that he headed toward. As options made themselves visible, he was able to check whether he'd still be able to see the mountain on that path. "I knew that as long as I kept walking towards the mountain I would be all right. And when I truly was not sure what to do, I could stop, and think about whether it was taking me towards or away from the mountain."

You might be thinking it's a tall order to figure out your mountain and start walking. You'd be right. I'm 46 while typing this, and I haven't properly figured out my mountain. I sort of have a small collection of mountains and some of them aren't even on the same continent. While I think it is important to think about your mountain, it can also be valuable (and easier) to figure out a few foothills and even some molehills.

You can set yourself a number of goals, both short term and long. They can be related to your personal life, schooling, career, skills, travel, or whatever you like. It's important to realize that goals are just that—things you'd like to achieve. Your life doesn't pass or fail based on whether you arrive at the mountain at a specific time. You should also keep in mind that working toward goals does not mean you can't be happy and content on the journey. Life is not about goals, it's about the journeys.

PLAN YOUR ROUTE

Goals are great. However, to paraphrase George Orwell's pigs from *Animal Farm*, all goals are equal, but some are more equal than others. Here are some ways to make your goals more equal.

Firstly, you need to recognize there are a number of components to the goal-setting process. You begin by deciding on a goal. Then you plan it, try it out, revise it, and work to achieve it. You can also cast it aside at any point of the process if it no longer makes sense for you.

Why do you want this goal? What benefits are there? What's the value? Do you know others who have achieved it? It's important to write it down. I am sure you hear that all the time. I do. There is something hard to describe in the experience of writing goals down on an actual piece of paper. It adds permanence and allows you to scribble other ideas down. It makes you stop brainstorming or daydreaming while you're in the act of putting pen to paper. It says, "okay, this is serious."

Step 1. Start now! Get out a pen and paper and brainstorm a list of goals.

They can be big (what do you want to be when you're older?), medium (is there somewhere specific you'd like to travel? Would you like to start a new activity?), or small (something you can accomplish today or tomorrow, like organizing your closet or cooking a meal). They can be serious or a little bit silly. Write down anything you might like to accomplish! No one has to see this paper but you. Then, pick one to start with.

Step 2. Now it's time to plan your goal.

But what are you supposed to be writing down? The first step of the planning is to make sure the goal is narrow. It has to be specific. Without a clear and concise goal, you can quickly feel stress and anxiety. The goal appears much larger and more difficult without that clarity.

Spend some time making a single sentence goal clear enough that someone else would immediately understand it. As an example, you may have written a goal like, "walk to a mountain." You can then refine it by naming which mountain, "walk to Mt. Fuji," and refine it further by naming the trail you will walk, "walk the Fujinomiya trail to the summit of Mt. Fuji." Getting more specific with each refinement, you may end up with a goal like, "walk the Fujinomiya trail to the summit of Mt. Fuji in the third week of July next year with Genevieve and Tracy."

Step 3. Now you need to make sure your goal stands up to a few requirements.

Using the same goal in step 2, here are a few questions that are helpful to ask when testing your goal:

- Is it achievable? Are you able to take time off in July? Are you physically able to make that climb? If Genevieve and Tracy can't come, is that a problem?
- Is there a time frame? Yes, it's in July.
- Will I know when I've succeeded? Yes, you'll be standing on top of Mt. Fuji live-streaming your awesomeness.

Once you've sorted this out it's time to get started. Take the first steps on the journey, see how it feels, figure out if it needs any changes or improvements. Maybe once you've spent a week talking to Genevieve and Tracy you realize that early August is probably going to work out better for everyone. Make the change and continue. Get your packing list together, figure out if the trip needs its own Instagram account, and start reading forums on the best ways to prepare for the climb.

Step 4. Make a list of people who might be able to help you.

Can you work with someone on your goal? Not necessarily have them go on the journey with you, but as someone you can check in with as you proceed. This could be a mentor or a friend.

Friends, teachers, family members? People from your Round Table or Hero Team? Make a list that you think works best for this specific goal. You can write why if you want, too, but you don't have to!

Step 5. Write down milestones and celebrate them.

What markers do you think you might pass on your way? Write these down—it's easier to feel good about your progress if you can see it happening. For something like cleaning a closet, it may just be steps on the process: *I got everything out of the closet. I filled one bag with trash.* For something like climbing Mt. Fuji, maybe it's starting research into trails and tours.

Try not to compete with someone else on the goal as it's easy to get discouraged if they're striding ahead. The only person you should compete with is the you of yesterday. Have you improved? Have you moved forward?

Make sure you're celebrating your successes. As you pass markers along the trail, give yourself a reward. It could be something tangible like a cake or a new pair of shoes. It could be just a slap on the back and an opportunity to recognize that you're doing well. It's important that we feel that our accomplishments are noteworthy. Recognizing big and small efforts will motivate you.

That's it. I want to achieve this specific goal. I will accomplish it by doing the following things. It will be done by a specific time. You can apply this to short term goals like, "I want to learn to play 'Wonderwall' in time for our campout." You can apply it to long term goals like, "I want to get a job teaching horses to swim by the time I'm 25."

But remember: It's okay to stop pursuing a goal. As you're working to achieve what you set out to do, it may stop being attractive. It might stop being possible. That's okay. If someone offers to take you to Paris in July, all expenses paid, then that would be a good reason to abandon the goal of going to Mt. Fuji in July.

⋙→ PUT IT ALL TOGETHER! ←⋘

Every journey needs an end goal! Some may be obvious and physical, like climbing Mt. Fuji. Some may be more personal, like learning a new skill or making new friends. Some may be short term, like acing a test, or they may be long-term, like becoming an architect. Whatever your goals are, remember:

- Planning and writing down your goals is one of the best ways to actually make them happen.

- Make sure your goals are specific, achievable, and measurable.

- It's okay for goals to change.

Okay, we've talked about heroes for five chapters now, and we still haven't talked about powers! Everyone has power—though in real life you're (probably) not going to be shooting webs from your wrists.

CHAPTER 6

WHAT IS YOUR POWER?

It's very easy to think that you're powerless in the world. How could little old you do anything to change anything? I hear it all the time. It's hard to imagine how one person could change a family or a school or a town or a nation. And yet it happens regularly. You'll find many examples of individuals changing the world in this book and internet will back me up with many more. The truth is that you do have power. There are many types of power that you can use to help make change. Here are some.

THE POWER OF SYMBOLS

It can be difficult to get your message out to people. One way to help with that is to use symbols. Wearing a rainbow pin on your shirt communicates to people that you're a member of the LGBTQ+ community (or an LGBTQ+ ally) without you having to say anything. Putting a peace sign bumper sticker on your car tells those following you on the highway that you're a fan of peace. Wearing a Manchester United shirt communicates that you have no taste and warns people not to talk to you about soccer (I jest. Maybe).

When Travis Price was in his final year of high school in Canada, he used the power of symbols to make a change in his school and then around the world. On the first day back from summer vacation, Travis and his friend, David, heard that a freshman boy had been crying at the end of the day out front of the school.

This kid had arrived for his first ever day of high school aiming to impress. He had worn new shoes, some cool jeans, and his favorite pink polo shirt. Before he even got in the front door, he received insults from students four years older than him. They had apparently decided that pink wasn't an appropriate color for boys to wear (as if colors belong to a specific gender!) and called him names. I won't type them here, but you can probably guess some of them. He got through this initial shocking welcome and went about figuring out how the high school schedule worked. When lunch arrived, he found those same senior students again. Or rather, they found him. This time they escalated. At one point one of them threatened to kill him if he ever wore pink to school again. This was his *first* day.

Word spread quickly and most people were laughing about the story on their way home. Travis and David had a different reaction. They were disappointed that this kid's first impression of the school, their school, was so negative. They decided to do something about it. Half an hour later, they had a plan—they were going to "unleash a sea of pink" across the school.

Their phones got a workout that night as they recruited all of their friends to wear a pink shirt the next day. Friends told other friends and Travis and David started to get excited. They realized that not everyone would have a pink shirt in their closet, so they worked with a local store to buy a box of shirts at a discount. The next day they stood out front of the school with their box of shirts and watched the tide of pink wash in. Two thirds of the student population wore pink to make the statement that no one at their school should be afraid to wear what they wanted. The kid who had experienced the worst day of his life on day one of high school had one of the best days of his life on day two.

Travis and David could not possibly have made such a statement without the power of symbols. This power drew attention from around the world as TV cameras turned up from as far away as New Zealand to report this amazing story. Other students started pink shirt days at their own schools. Workplaces did the same. These two kids had used the power of symbols to spread a message around the world. Travis now runs Pink Shirt Day every year at the end of February with hundreds of thousands of people joining in. He's also a full-time public speaker who uses his story to motivate others.

Symbols can communicate quickly. They can spread a message great distances. They can speak across languages.

Bree Newsome knew the power of symbols when she climbed a flagpole to remove the Confederate flag. Rosa Parks knew the power of symbols when she sat in the "wrong" seat on a bus. What change could you make using the power of symbols?

THE POWER OF SOCIAL MEDIA

Social media is a terrible curse inflicted upon the youth of the world that is destroying their moral character as much as their attention spans. Or not. Social media is a popular punching bag for people who like to complain. There's no doubt it is a tool that can be used for evil or general mischief, but it's still just a tool. For every livestreaming of a high school brawl there's a fundraising campaign that changes the life of someone injured in a high school brawl. The power of social media comes from its ability to amplify.

In high school, Jeremiah Anthony found himself sitting in the school auditorium listening to yet another anti-bullying speech. An outside speaker was boring the audience with episodes of bullying from her childhood. The message is always the same with these kinds of talks—I'm sure you've heard plenty of them. The speaker thinks that if they tell you enough stories about how bullying hurt them, you'll see the light and stop bullying people.

Jeremiah could sense the restlessness among the thousand students around him. Then the speaker got his attention. "Do you want to know how to stop bullying?" Everyone leaned forward waiting to hear the solution. "Don't be a bully." That was it. That was her magical insight. As one, the crowd burst out laughing. The assembly was quickly ended by the principal and students were ushered out. To most of the students, this was an amusing distraction. For Jeremiah, it was thought provoking. This "bullying expert" didn't know the solution, so what was it? The words of his first-grade teacher suddenly leapt into his mind. She had told the class that people who bully have low self-esteem. So, was that the solution? Just increase everyone's self-esteem? He figured he'd give it a try.

With a couple of friends, Jeremiah created the handle @westhighbros on Twitter to start paying compliments to students at West High School. The tweets went to a specific person, picked at random, with a clear compliment. For example, one was "You make everyone happy with your quirkiness."

The founders had to be careful not to favor anyone, and being tenth graders helped. Seniors may have been tempted to focus on themselves or perhaps not even remember that other students existed at the school. Freshman may not have received any attention. Due to their diligence and forethought, the three boys created a Twitter account that everyone at the school followed, waiting for their compliment to arrive. With more than a thousand students at the school, Jeremiah had to recruit even more tweeters to the team. Self-esteem increased and bullying decreased. Success.

Without the Twitter account, this plan would have been a lot more difficult. Walking the halls handing out compliments would have been more time-consuming, more awkward, and more likely to fail. Social media allows you to reach an audience more quickly and broadly.

Word got out about the project and soon national TV coverage came to this Iowa school. When the cameras arrived, the staff at the school were surprised. They didn't know anything about @westhighbros. These students had imagined, planned, and executed an anti-bullying program without involving the staff. It goes to show that if you want to make a change in your school or community, you can do it without permission and use the power of social media to make it work.

THE POWER OF REAL COOL

I went to school with a girl named Jodie. She wasn't one of the glamorous kids and wasn't one of the rebels. She was Jodie. She did all the little things right. She didn't call you a friend one day and an enemy the next, she didn't call people names behind their backs. In short, she didn't do what a lot of people do in high school. She was Jodie. She knew all of the cool music before it was cool. She would talk to you like you were a real person, not someone with numerous stigmas hanging over your head. Of course, I was in high school and barely noticed any of that. I was killing myself trying to get noticed by the glamorous kids and rebels.

CHECK OUT THE SCIENCE!
Social Media and Civic Engagement

Civic engagement is things like writing to public officials, giving money to a candidate or cause, working for political campaigns, voting in elections, and doing community service. Social media has a big effect on how involved in our communities we are—but it's not enough to have access to social media. We need to know how to find *accurate* information. That's called **media literacy,** and studies have shown that people are much more likely to spread positive messages and engage positively in their community if they're better at this. Good media literacy basically just means paying attention to content. Don't just skim headlines; learn how to compare sources, understand the main points of articles, and form your own opinions based on facts. It's those critical thinking skills teachers are always pushing!

Jodie had **Real Cool**. She wasn't popular because she worked on it every day. She didn't get popular by attacking those around her, trying to push them down the pecking order. In fact, she was popular because she *wasn't* doing those things. Her Real Cool came from not trying to be cool. Jodie was comfortable being Jodie and it showed.

You might know someone like Jodie. Other people flock to them hoping some of the cool rubs off. When Jodie liked a band, everyone else liked that band, but she never liked a band because other people liked it. It seemed like magic to me.

In 2011, *The New York Times* reported on some new research on bullying in schools. Their big discovery was that most bullying and aggressive behavior was happening in the top half of the social pecking order. This was counter to what most adults thought, because they'd been raised on '80s movies where the bully was always some oafish, popular villain who picked on the lower-status hero of the story. It's unlikely to be surprising to you though, because you're probably living in that world right now. Bullying is designed to help lift people up the pecking order—or more accurately, it's used to push others down. Bullying is nearly always about status.

What was interesting to me, and got pushed down the story a bit, was that the top two percent of students in terms of popularity exhibited the least amount of bullying or aggressive activity. I'd guess that some of those students realized that to stay at the top they had to tone down the aggression. They could allow their minions to do the dirty work. The rest were presumably popular because of Real Cool.

The Real Cool kids have the power to change things. So much of the student body looks up to them and often mimics them. This influence isn't dependent on fear. It comes from people genuinely admiring them and wondering how they too could care so little about what others think about them.

The problem is that this small percentage of people rarely recognize that they possess the power of Real Cool. When they do, great things can happen. Jeremiah would not have succeeded if he didn't have Real Cool. The students at Travis's school would not have followed along if they thought he was trying to benefit from his actions. Jodie didn't think she was anything special. She told me a few years ago that my description of her didn't match her own impression. She was

CHECK OUT THE SCIENCE!
Research Report, Bullying and Status

Scientists followed students in North Carolina for three years to see how their aggressive behavior affected their social status over time. They watched everything from physical aggression like hitting and shoving, to verbal and emotional aggression, like calling people names or spreading rumors. They found people who were trying to change their social status—who wanted to move up the social ladder—used aggression to do it. But people at the top and bottom of the hierarchy didn't. Of course, how supportive friends in each group were affected this, but the idea that those at the top *don't* act aggressively was pretty surprising!

dealing with many common emotions during her teenage years: anxiety, depression, fear of missing out. But she didn't turn them into outwardly negative behaviors, so she appeared to be cool, calm, and collected.

If we want to create real change in schools and communities, the people with the power of Real Cool can lead the way. We just have to convince them. Perhaps you're someone with Real Cool or perhaps you are friends with someone who has it. Being deliberate about your actions can bring about change. One school counsellor in Texas recognized that.

Carri Elliot met with a high school student who had been abused during school hours and at the bus stop. He had just found his locker broken into and his shoes missing. He was desperate. In fact, he told her that he prayed every morning for a good day. The prayers hadn't been working. Carri approached the kids who were targeting the freshman but they basically laughed and then accused him of squealing. The situation did not improve, as you can imagine.

Recognizing how much social status came from football in Texas, Carri recruited three varsity football players to meet the boy at his locker each break and then to escort him to his class. The bullying stopped instantly. The football players basically hung out with him, chatting and joking while walking with him. It was a complete success. Carri expanded the program by recruiting a dozen other football players.

Now, I'm sure the fact that these football players were basically giants and their status as idols helped, but it was their lack of concern about that status that gave them the power of Real Cool and enabled a peaceful solution to the problem this freshman (and many others) experienced. If they'd used their size and status to threaten the bullies, it would have reinforced the mean behavior and nothing would have changed.

THE POWER OF PEER PRESSURE

Peer pressure. It's famous for making teens do bad things and has been for decades. Smoking, drinking, sex, drugs, vandalism, and more. Old people use the term in the negative. "Oh, my kid is doing something bad? Must be peer pressure." "Watch out for peer pressure kids!"

However, the words "peer" and "pressure" aren't inherently negative. Put together, they simply mean the urge to do what other people like you are doing. If all of the people you hang out with are wearing green pants, then you will feel pressure to go shopping for some leafy pants. It's normal. You want to fit in.

It comes from that same idea of social groups and norms we discussed earlier.

If all of your friends are doing good things, you'll feel the same pull. If they're all volunteering at a soup kitchen on Saturdays, then it's likely you'll soon be similarly busy on Saturdays.

When I worked at camp, one of our new staff members would always pick up trash if she saw some while walking around. It didn't matter if you were in a deep conversation with her, she'd stop and pick up the chip bag or paper cup. She was a really nice person and someone people wanted to be close to. She had Real Cool. Naturally, other people started picking up trash as they walked the camp too. Pretty soon nearly everyone was doing it without even thinking about it. Once it got to that stage, it had morphed from the power of Real Cool to the power of Peer Pressure. Any new staff member coming into our camp noticed that everyone was picking up trash when they saw it. So, obviously they did too. It became a norm.

Norms, like peer pressure, can be negative or positive. As discussed earlier, norms can exist because of misconceptions. Just because we think everyone is drinking doesn't mean they are. There's an easy way to overcome this perception problem: Just ask everyone. The schools in Brighton, Michigan, did just that. They asked all of the students to anonymously give their opinions on bullying, name-calling, racism, drug-taking, and more. They collated all of the answers and made posters to put up all around the schools. It showed that high percentages of students disapproved of all of those things. Duh. As a result, the percentage of students actually doing those things fell. Once people knew what the norms were, they fit their behavior to them. The same thing has happened in dozens of college campuses around the country when looking at the norms of alcohol abuse. When presented with the actual norms, the problems related to binge drinking dropped every time.

The book *Schooled*, by Gordon Korman, illustrates the power of norms well. Capricorn Anderson, a life-long home-schooled kid, is forced to start attending school. He is nice to everyone, enjoys learning, and dresses how he likes. All of these things are against the norms of the school. He refuses to be changed by the school and, eventually, most of the other students realize they don't actually agree with the norms either. In the end (spoiler alert), the norms of the school change to match those of the majority, led by Capricorn's example. It takes a strong-willed and confident person to lead that kind of change, but maybe you're the one to do it in your groups.

You can use peer pressure and norms to amplify your power to make positive change. If you can get a large group of people to act in a certain way, you will get even more people to act that way. Likewise, if you can get a large group of people to *think* that most people act a certain way, then you'll have the same effect.

THE POWER OF ACTION

> "Good actions give strength to ourselves and inspire good actions in others."—Plato

Doing good is doubly good if it's inspiring good actions in others, and it may come around to you a third time! It's a great value investment. You've heard the saying "actions speak louder than words," I'm sure. Action communicates in a very direct way. It says, "This is how you do it!"

I don't want to argue with Plato, but I think there's an even more valuable aspect of taking good action. When you perform a positive act for someone else, especially a heroic act, it tells that person that you care. That may seem trivial compared with Plato's statement, but I believe it can have a much deeper impact.

In the last ten years, teen suicide from bullying has been increasingly visible. That may be because it's happening more or perhaps because there are so many more media channels broadcasting 24 hours a day. In the vast majority of cases, the suicide victim has felt alone. They think no one cares about them, so they assume that no one will care if they live or die. This loneliness comes from feeling that no one takes action to support them. They don't sense that anyone cares. Action can change that. Let's also be clear: It's not uncommon for people who have support to feel that they don't, or that the support isn't enough. Showing it more can only help.

Action can be scary. And it can be hard to do. We often make it even harder on ourselves by assuming that there is only one course of action. If we see someone being picked on, we think we have to get in the bully's face. If we come upon someone drowning in a swollen river, we figure we're going to get wet. It's rare that there's only one option, though. We could offer support to the target of the bullying after the fact. We could call emergency services for the person in the river.

> **"Don't let what you cannot do interfere with what you can do."—John Wooden**

When he was ten years old, Ethan King went to Mozambique on a trip with his father. His dad was helping build wells in remote villages to provide safe drinking water. Ethan went along to experience life in a place different to his western

Michigan home. He did take one thing to remind him of home, though—his soccer ball. Ethan lived and breathed soccer, so it was impossible to imagine two weeks without playing. He figured there would have to be at least a couple of kids to play with where he was headed.

Two weeks later, when it was time to leave, Ethan had to say goodbye, not to a couple of new friends, but to dozens, from villages near and far, who had come to play with him every day.

On the first day, a couple of kids had indeed been interested in playing. When they saw Ethan's new ball, they were amazed. Despite playing soccer every day for as long as they could remember, neither of the kids had ever seen a real ball. They had used rolled up plastic bags for their ball because money had to be used for more important things like food and shelter. It certainly hadn't stopped them from playing, but to finally see a real ball was a thrill. Word spread and the playing group grew every day.

When it came time to say goodbye, Ethan gave his ball to his new friends so they could enjoy it without him. He had plenty of other balls at home, so it was not a big deal to him. To those kids, it meant a lot. Their joyful faces stayed with him for a long time.

On the flight home, Ethan couldn't shake that image. He started thinking about how he could make it happen again. An idea was born on that long trip home in airports and inside planes. The plan for Charity Ball was hatched when he arrived in Michigan.

Ethan started a nonprofit organization at age 10. Charity Ball sends new, good-quality soccer balls to kids in need around the world. From Ethan's initial small act came the larger act of committing his time and effort to a nonprofit and a family of supporters dedicated to showing kids around the world that they care. It produces smiles just like those that

Ethan saw in Mozambique the first time. Those smiles come from knowing that someone, somewhere in the world, cares.

Ethan took action when he saw a problem, but he had plenty of time to take that action—and he is still taking it years later. A lot of heroes don't have time, as we saw in the second definition chapter. The Reaction Hero has to do something now or not at all.

That restriction of time can also restrict our awareness of the options available to us. When confronted with a need for action we can think in binary terms—either we do the big scary thing or nothing at all. That kid is getting beaten up? Have to get in there to break it up, but that's scary, so I'll do nothing. That man is drowning in the river? Have to jump in and swim over to rescue him, but that's scary, so I'll do nothing. The truth is there is always a range of opportunities. Get help, offer support, call the authorities. Something is better than nothing.

Your most common opportunities to act heroically are in social situations. So, apart from the obvious scary option of standing up to the aggressor, what can you do?

Grab the attention of aggressor. Anything that diverts from the target is going to be helpful. If you keep it non-confrontational, it's easier for you. Easier makes it more likely that you'll do it, right? You could tell them to chill out. You could ask them why they're doing it. These options might not work—there may be no chilling or explaining—but the diversion can help deescalate the situation or let the target get away from the immediate threat.

Connect with the target of the behavior. This could be while the attack is happening through eye contact or shrugging your shoulders. Give them a sympathetic smile or mouth some supportive words. Letting them know you're aware of what's happening and that you don't approve of it can help. Support them afterwards, as well. A nod in the hall can make someone's day. Ask them to join you at lunch. Like the recipients of balls from Charity Ball, the connection shows that someone cares.

Be an active witness. That could be done by interacting with bystanders, encouraging them to say something or walk away. You can even communicate with your body language. It could be that you record what's happening to help back up the target in case it becomes a "his word versus mine" problem. Being active could also mean getting the attention of authority figures. That could be a teacher, someone higher up the pecking order, or a friend of the aggressor or target.

Action shows others that we care. That action can be performed in many ways, in various levels of scary. It can be done with time or without it. It just needs to be done. A display of caring can be life-changing in the right situation.

THE POWER OF PRIVILEGE

Many problems are big. Bigger than you can probably imagine. They're built into the way we do everyday things. It's not like everyone gets up each morning and makes a decision to destroy the environment or repress minorities. The way politics works, the way business works, the way school works; all of them create and maintain many problems. Privilege is one of those problems. Those who are part of the dominant group benefit from the way the systems (usually created by the dominant group) benefit them. Most of the dominant group are completely oblivious to all of the ways those systems give them advantages.

Many people react negatively to the idea that they're privileged. It makes them think of fancy upper class people with English accents living in a large country home with silver spoons and pet corgis. People say to themselves, "I've worked hard to get where I am!" And they might be right.

However, two different people working exactly as hard as each other will get different results based on their level of systemic privilege.

If the crayon labeled "flesh" is the same color as your skin, that's privilege. If all of the people on TV look like you, that's privilege. If everyone around you worships the same god as you, that's privilege. It doesn't feel like privilege to you, because it's normal. You're unlikely to even notice. It's impossible not to notice for the many people who are different to you. Imagine never seeing someone like you in a movie. How would that feel? Some of you don't need to imagine.

It takes a lot of time and a lot of people to dismantle the structures that exist. It can feel impossible to change, but as a budding hero, that is no obstacle to you. Hopefully you've already seen that one person or a small group can make a difference. If you're one of the people benefiting from the way things work, it's up to you to work against it.

Sophie Scholl was a white German teenager living during Adolf Hitler's rise to power. She had privilege. She joined the Hitler Youth, thinking that she was helping Germany achieve a glorious future. It didn't take her too long to realize she was wrong. Rather than stay safe as one of the privileged majority, she and a group of friends started a group called The White Rose. They created leaflets and graffiti campaigns to explain the many problems created by the Hitler regime. They were ultimately unsuccessful in toppling Hitler (they weren't the only ones), but they did make an impact.

You can start to use the power of privilege by educating yourself about ways that you receive advantages from the culture you live in. Learn about the problems facing those around you that are lacking privilege. It can be pretty uncomfortable to realize what you didn't know. Learn it anyway. There are others who will benefit from your knowledge.

Don't take it personally. You didn't create the structure that lifted you above others. Make sure you're listening to those without that privilege. They often have trouble getting heard. Maybe you can help share their words as people with the same privilege as you are more likely to listen to you. Then you can start using your position to help level the playing field.

There are opportunities to do this every day. It could be as simple as speaking up when you see a classmate being treated poorly because of how they look. It can be letting someone know you are there to support them when they're being unjustly treated by the police or store staff and recording it on your phone. You could make sure the rules and regulations of your school are not being accidentally (or deliberately) unfair to a minority group. It can be simple or it can be difficult. It can be scary and risky. It can be heroic.

ᐯᐯ⟶ PUT IT ALL TOGETHER! ⟵ᐯᐯ

Was that what you expected in a chapter on hero powers? Maybe not, but these real-life powers are important.

- Power comes in many forms, from many places.

- Some power is obvious, like symbols, peer pressure, and action. Some is harder to see, like attitudes and privilege.

- Pay attention to the power you have and how you're using it—are you using your power for good or evil?

So now we know the steps, the people, the goals, and the powers. How do we put it all together and actually become the hero of our own story?

CHAPTER 7

CAN YOU BE A HERO?

"To be in good moral condition requires at least as much training as to be in good physical condition."
—Jawaharlal Nehru

There's no guarantee that you'll use the power you have and do the right thing, of course. People regularly assume they will, but when the situation arises, they're stuck as bystanders. It's almost like these situations make us roll the dice to see if we act or remain frozen. Or maybe more like throwing a dart at a board.

Imagine a dart board with three sections. The biggest section takes up three quarters of the board—it's huge. It is hard to avoid hitting that section. Let's call it the "Do Nothing" section. Then there's a "Do Good" section that's about one fifth of the board. The third section is a sliver and we'll call it the "Do Bad" section. Don't get caught up on the exact numbers—this is a board for the everyday person on the street. Yours will be different—maybe by a lot, maybe by a little.

When we're confronted with a situation that wants action from us, our brain throws a dart at this board. Blindfolded. Most of the time we do nothing. Sometimes we do good. Sometimes we do bad.

When you hear someone being made fun of, for example, your brain throws a dart. Do nothing or do something. Most of time you ignore the meanness and get on with your day. Sometimes you'll tell the person to stop, or you'll offer support to the target. Sometimes you might throw out a joke of your own.

The good news is that your dart board can be changed. It can change temporarily in the moment based on the situation. For example, if you're surrounded by friends, your "Do Good" section is bigger than normal while they're there because you know they'll support you. Maybe there's a big crowd of strangers so your "Do Good" section shrinks for a while.

The best kind of change is more permanent. If your "Do Good" section is three quarters of the dart board normally, then even if the person who needs your help is a stranger, there's still a great chance you'll do the right thing. This kind of change comes from training.

The Greek warrior poet Archilochus (sounds like a great Dungeons & Dragons character) knew all about how we react to situations. He said, "We don't rise to the level of our expectations, we fall to the level of our training." He means that all the good intentions in the world don't matter when a situation is slapping us right in the face demanding a response. We do what we're trained to do. If we're not trained to do the right thing, then we're unlikely to.

We've already gone over the things that contribute to our "Do Nothing" section. Let's start with what we can do to make our "Do Good" section big.

WHO, ME?

It's easy to say, "I could never be a hero." Maybe you don't think you're strong enough or brave enough or smart enough. Maybe you think you've done too many bad things in the past to be able to do a good thing tomorrow. But heroes are born from action, not reputation or ability.

In 2005, Jabbar Gibson performed an act that no-one would have predicted based on his past and no one would guess now based on his present. He grew up in the Fischer Projects in New Orleans. He was kicked out of high school in tenth grade for fighting, and started making money with drugs and odd jobs.

Jabbar was 20 years old in the summer of 2005. He was arrested for possession of crack cocaine in June and again for a high-speed car chase that resulted in a number of injuries to police in August. Hurricane Katrina arrived in the last days of August, and the projects that Jabbar called home were hit hard.

After surviving the initial storm, Jabbar and his friends realized that they needed to get out. Their homes were severely damaged, the power was out, and they had heard the rivers were about to break. After siphoning some gas from abandoned gas stations, they discovered a school bus depot and Jabbar decided to steal one of the buses. He had no idea how to drive a bus and had no way to know whether the bus was in need of repairs. But he saw no other option. Word spread quickly and suddenly Jabbar was the captain of a rescue bus filled with 60 people.

After navigating through two encounters with police, Jabbar led his merry crew to Texas. They stopped to pick people up on the way and Jabbar spent more than $1,000 on food and supplies. Eventually they made it to the Astrodome in Houston where everyone was given food and shelter. Jabbar became famous overnight.

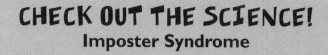

CHECK OUT THE SCIENCE!
Imposter Syndrome

Imposter syndrome is when people feel like they are, well, imposters. Like they aren't really the people others think they are and somehow they've fooled everyone, and they're bound to let everyone down eventually when they are exposed for who they truly are. Some high-achievers feel like they can't live up to others' expectations of them, that they're not capable or talented (even though they are). You might be shocked to realize just how many "heroes" constantly doubt themselves.

People with imposter syndrome see any one failure and mistake as proof that they don't belong where they are, and any successes were just flukes, or luck. Have you ever felt like a total fake or fraud? About school, or your friends, or even your family? It's common, and it's important to remember that it's not true. The best remedy is consistent, clear support from family and friends; talk to them about your worries! You might be amazed at some of the things they have to say. And if you have a friend or family member who has this sort of anxiety, you can help them by doing the same; talk to them, tell them all the things you like about them, and recognize their accomplishments.

In 2010, Jabbar was imprisoned for possession of guns and drugs. After his heroism, he'd met Oprah, Will Smith, and many more celebrities who celebrated his actions. None of that stopped him from committing more crimes. After his 15-year sentence was reduced to 5, he left prison and moved to Baton Rouge. And no, he's not a bus driver.

If your head is telling you that you've done too many bad things in the past to be a hero, think about Jabbar. If you're thinking heroes have to do the right thing every day, think about Jabbar. If you think you don't have the skills to be a hero, think about Jabbar. Not because his life should necessarily be an inspiration—but because being heroic doesn't have to be a constant state. You don't have to be perfect to be heroic (we discussed this earlier!). Never doubt that you can do heroic things, no matter how many mistakes you've made in the past.

Thinking that you could never be a hero is a **fixed mindset.** We all have areas in life that we believe we can't improve in. How often do you hear people say, "I'm just not a math person" or "I'm not a good swimmer"? In saying these types of things, our mindset is that we're born that way, that our level of ability or skill is fixed in place. That's a fixed mindset. It also happens with positive statements, "I'm a natural runner" or "I was born an artist." This kind of thinking is limiting, of course. If you think you're not a math person, then you're unlikely to try to improve. If you think you could never be a hero, then you're unlikely to try. It can even be limiting the other way: If you think you were born to be or do something, any lack of success in that area may be way more soul-crushing than it needs to be.

The opposite of a fixed mindset is a **growth mindset.** If your attitude to anything is that you can improve by practicing and putting effort in, then you're willing to try new things. Psychologist Carol Dweck is a leading thinker in this field.

She suggests that if you ever find yourself thinking, "I can't do that," you should add the word "yet" to the end.

I'm not good enough to write a book. Yet.

I can't do this kind of math. Yet.

I'm not the kind of person who could be a hero. Yet.

THE LITTLE THINGS (THE HEROIC HABIT)

At the end of the 1900s, St. Therese (not to be confused with St. (Mother) Teresa from earlier!) wrote about her **"Little Way."** Her theory was that people could get close to God through performing little acts every day, rather than large displays of devotion or performing miracles. This kind of habit created a mindset that allowed for normal people to aim for heaven. It was a revolutionary idea for the Christian church at that time.

Similarly, most heroism is more about the small actions done every day in preparation to act when the big events occur. These are **Heroic Habits.** When we hear about heroes, images of the famous world-changers often come to mind, but the truth is that heroic acts come from the accumulation of little things done regularly. It's the accumulation that changes the world.

> **"Few will have the greatness to bend history itself; but each of us can work to change a small portion of events, and in the total of all those acts will be written the history of this generation."—Robert Kennedy**

People often ask me if a certain act is heroic. Most of the time they're asking about something that is simply a good thing. Is picking up trash in my neighborhood heroic? No,

CHECK OUT THE SCIENCE!
Growth and Fixed Mindsets

Mindsets are how people think about their own abilities. There are two main ones: growth and fixed.

A growth mindset is when you believe that your abilities can be built, strengthened, or expanded—basically, that you can get better at something! A fixed mindset is the belief that your abilities can't be changed or improved—you either have the skill or you don't, and it will always be like that. Like when people say "I'm just not an artist" or "I'm just not good at math." They don't bother to practice or get help because they think it's pointless and they'll never get better. But someone with a growth mindset is okay with practicing, seeking help, and failing a few times on the way to getting better.

As you've probably guessed, a growth mindset is much more helpful and likely to result in success. Try actively challenging your assumptions about your abilities—you might be amazed at what you can accomplish!

but it's a good example for others and improves everyone's mood to live in a tidy place. Is smiling at people every day heroic? No, but it is going to increase your connection with people and improve happiness in others. Hero training, in general, isn't heroic. It's a series of practices that make you more likely to be the hero in a difficult situation. However, those practices will also make you a better person and improve the world around you.

One of these practices is to give a compliment every day. Compliments are difficult. They open you up. People are usually suspicious of compliments from strangers, so you're naturally nervous right before you give one. Do it anyway. For you, it's a way to get used to interacting with strangers and to pay attention to the people around you. Remember that you have to notice a need before you can be a hero to someone. For them, it's going to make them feel good, even if just for a second. More than likely that feeling will last a day and perhaps longer. I am currently wearing a pair of shoes that I bought after my previous pair got a hole in the sole. I had little choice in the shoe store and had to buy right then (it was pouring rain). I ended up with a pair that didn't really fit how I see myself. They had a bit of flair to them, while I usually go for plain black. I received so many compliments about them over the last two years that I am now obsessed with trying to find a similarly cool pair of shoes, because these have holes in the soles again. I've needed new shoes for three months, but compliments from strangers have stuck with me so much that I can't bring myself to buy a new, less-cool pair.

St. Therese had her "Little Way" and you can too. Paying compliments and picking up trash are good ideas to start. What can you add? Think about your average day. Where are there opportunities for you to do something little that could turn into a habit and end up making a big difference in the world?

There is a strength in making these little things habits. There are hundreds of books on how to build habits, how to stop habits, and how habits help. A lot of people consider habits to be bad—almost like "bad habit" is one word. They talk about smoking, gambling, picking your nose, etc. But we have plenty of good habits that we probably don't even notice. Habits make life easier. For example, I brush my teeth exactly the same way every morning. I start at the front, bottom, left, and work to the right, then back across the top, then back once more at the back. Then I move to the top and repeat. The brush angle is the same every time, changing as I move around my mouth. If I get interrupted, I can't just start from where I left off. It feels weird. This is an extreme habit. I've been brushing my teeth every day for a long time and so it's a habit that I don't even think about and which feels weird when interrupted.

I have other habits that feel weird when broken. I shower every morning. I know in my head that it's possible to go without a shower for a day, but I feel mentally uncomfortable for hours if I get up and don't shower right away. You should aim to create hero-habits like this; they're super strong. If you can get to the point where you feel weird without complimenting someone every day, you're going to be in good shape when someone needs a hero.

> "We are what we repeatedly do. Excellence, then, is not an act but a habit."—Aristotle

Aristotle was all over this more than 2,000 years ago. I'd say heroism is an act built by habit. Start your habits today.

BEATING FEAR

Fear is something most people face, yet there are many ways to face it. Fear can be avoided, ignored, enhanced, minimized, examined, and faced head on.

CHECK OUT THE SCIENCE!
Forming Habits

You might have heard of Pavlov's dogs: they developed a habit of drooling at the sound of a bell because each time they were fed, they heard that sound. The dogs' brains made the connection between the sound and the food. This is called **classical conditioning.** Lots of habits are classically conditioned responses that we have learned over time. A habit can be as simple as checking for texts every time you pick up your phone, or opening the fridge every time you enter the kitchen, even if you're not hungry. Your brain has just learned to do these things, and does them automatically now (sound familiar?).

To break habits, you need to re-train your brain. This can be hard because your brain and body are so used to doing the habit. The best way to break a habit is to replace it with a new action: maybe each time you walk into the kitchen, you make a point to check the clock on the microwave rather than opening the fridge. And you can build good habits the same way— it starts out intentional, and eventually it becomes automatic. Once again: it's all brain training!

Fear has been a vital piece of our survival tools since the beginning of humanity. It kept us safe in a dangerous world. Today is the safest the world had ever been, but fear has stuck with us. While it hasn't become useless, it's a lot less useful than it used to be and has started getting in the way of our day to day lives. It has certainly become a large obstacle to heroic action as our brain uses it as a contradicting voice. What if the bully picks on me? What if I start drowning? What if I lose my friends?

> "Can a man still be brave if he's afraid?"—Bran Stark
> "That is the only time a man can be brave."
> —Eddard Stark

The Parkour expert and teacher, Dan Edwardes, suggests that fear is built up into a complicated structure from when we're young and told not to climb because we might fall, to avoid strangers because they're out to get you, and other such overstated risks. The more we add to the structure over our lives, the harder it is to ignore. The good news is that because the structure is built, we can dismantle it.

> "Every fear is learned through experience. In fact, only two are hard-wired into the brain: the fear of falling (not to be confused with the fear of heights) and the fear of loud noises. All other fears we acquire and reinforce over time."—Dan Edwardes

Dan's solution is to do things that scare you. He does this through Parkour in his native London. The jumps and maneuvers that he performs on a regular basis allow him to observe and overcome fear. His suggestion for deliberate practice is broken down into three parts: observing the fear, taking action to move past it, and focusing on the specific task that is provoking the fear. For example, when planning to jump from one building to another, Dan will take a moment to observe the fear that is suggesting to his brain that he avoid this at all costs. Then he'll take action to confront and bypass the fear, usually by taking some deep, controlled breaths. Finally, he'll focus on exactly how the jump will be performed; the steps, the foot he'll take off with, and how and where he'll land.

Because he's deliberately performing this kind of process often, he can use those three steps in other places where he might feel fear. He can observe, act, and focus when asking a girl out on a date, or giving a talk on a big stage, or admitting to a group of strangers that he loved Batman vs. Superman: Dawn of Justice.

> **"We suffer more in imagination than in reality."**
> **—Seneca**

Our imagination has created the scaffolding of fear that Dan described. One way to destabilize that scaffolding is to do the practical exercises that Dan suggests. Another is to shine the light of reality onto those imaginings. Author Tim Ferriss suggests an activity called **Fear Setting**. In it, he asks you to confront the fear around a decision. The first step is to define the fear around the decision. What are all the bad things that could happen if you did this thing? The second step is to figure out what you could do to prevent the negative outcomes you listed in the first part. The third is to figure out what you could do if the bad thing happens. Who would you ask for help, how could you fix the issue, or how have other people solved the problem? After this breakdown, you should ask yourself what benefits could come from taking this action and what could be the negative effects of not taking it.

The night before I first went to Paris (this was before easy access to the internet), I was crying from fear. The person

CHECK OUT THE SCIENCE!
Fear and the Brain

Fear is based in the part of the brain called the **amygdala**. When our senses detect danger, our amygdala reacts even before we have time to think about it. Snakes, cars moving erratically, heights—these are all things that our brains interpret instinctively as DANGER! Fear is also linked to memory, which is good because it means we can react even quicker next time. But it also makes fears hard to get rid of. We have to work extra hard to re-train our brain that something is not as dangerous as our instincts say. Imagine learning to dive off a high dive. It's scary the first time! Our brain tells us that heights are dangerous! But once our brain learns it's not so dangerous after all, it stops triggering such an intense fear response. Even just imagining the situation, or paying attention to other people who have done it, can help our brain learn. You can even try it for heroism; preparing your brain will reduce your fear of action when the moment comes.

I was planning to stay with hadn't answered the phone in two weeks. I didn't speak French apart from a few words I knew from watching a French TV show. I didn't have any French currency. It was going to be nighttime when I arrived. I wasn't sure how exactly I was supposed to get from the ferry to the train once I'd crossed the English Channel.

One by one, those fears disappeared. On the ferry I exchanged some English Pounds to French francs and managed to figure out what that would be in Australian

Dollars. I simply followed the crowd from the ferry to the train station. Once on the train, I encountered something that Tim, in his TED Talk, describes as a useful tool.

There were three very loud Englishmen on the carriage with me. They were angry because they felt the francs they'd received were lower than they were supposed to be. They were doing the math wrong. There were a number of smiles around the carriage while some friendly people tried to explain that everything was done fairly. Someone asked them why they were headed to Paris and they replied that they were going to watch a horse race. They said they had no idea where the racecourse was, but that was okay because they were meeting a friend. "Where are you meeting your friend?" someone asked. "Oh, next to a big arch thing." The Arc de Triomphe. "Do you know how to get there?" They had no idea, but they figured it would be hard not to notice a big arch thing.

This interaction made me realize that millions of people arrived in Paris every year worse prepared than I was and survived the experience. Tim Ferriss suggests that you ask yourself if less prepared, less confident, or less intelligent people have done this before and pulled it off. The answer is likely to be yes. And if not, you have the luxury to prepare yourself better.

LOOK OUTSIDE

To avoid being stuck in our own little world, we need to practice looking out of ourselves. As we've seen, the first requirement of acting heroically is that you notice a need. If you don't look, you won't see.

Practice taking a minute to notice everything going on around you. A full minute—set a timer. Pay attention to the sounds, sights, smells. Who is saying what? Who is doing what? What can you tell about body language?

Can you make any predictions about what might happen next? Is there a chance that girl over there is going to trip on the uneven tile? Is that old man unaware of the motorcycle that's darting between traffic?

What would you do if one of those things did happen? Stretch it out. If the girl did trip, she might fall and start bleeding. What's the first step? Then what? And then what? If you've already walked through what you'd do, you're more likely to do it if the need arises.

A great way to enhance your attention is to practice meditation. Meditation and mindfulness are pretty popular in lots of settings. Both of these practices can improve issues with stress and anxiety, increase focus, make you sleep better, and even give you a healthier body. Those are all good things. However, there are a couple of things that can directly help with your hero training.

David DeSteno is a psychology professor and author. His research suggests that meditation can help with compassionate helping behavior. The first way is through meditation's ability to improve our attention to the world around us. He argues that if we are aware of someone in need, we're more likely to help them. Sound familiar?

The second part is that meditation teaches us that we're all connected. We're more likely to help those we feel a connection to. We saw that in the social groups chapter. DeSteno has seen in experiments that we feel more compassion towards people who are also simply tapping their hands together, if we're also doing it. Hardly a strong connection! If, through regularly meditating, we can feel that kind of connection to those around us, then we're much more likely to help.

There are plenty of places to find ways to meditate. You could ask a teacher, get online, or use an app. If that seems like

CHECK OUT THE SCIENCE!
Meditation and Helping Behavior

In one study, DeSteno set up an experiment where a group of 20 people participated in an eight-week meditation course, and another group of 20 did not. After those eight weeks, participants were brought to a room thinking they would be taking a written test but were really being tested on their helping behavior. While the participant was sitting waiting for their test, a person who appeared to be in distress and had difficulty walking entered the room and leaned against the wall—because the only chair in the room was the one the participant was sitting in. The scientists found that 15% of people who did not meditate got up and offered their seat to this person . . . but 50% of the people who meditated offered their seat.

too much work, then simply do the one-minute observation every day. Just stop and really pay attention to everything around you for one minute. You'll be surprised how quickly it becomes a habit that you don't even notice.

HEROIC IMAGINATION

> "Everything you can imagine is real."
> —Pablo Picasso

Zeno Franco and Philip Zimbardo coined the term **"heroic imagination"** in 2006. I took it to mean that we should regularly imagine ourselves as the hero in various situations.

If we imagine ourselves as heroes, then we're more likely to perform heroic actions. I'm sure Picasso was thinking of something else, but his words apply to the heroic imagination.

My imagination was always running when I was a kid. I'm not sure it has stopped, to be honest. Once, in eleventh grade, it came in particularly handy. We were at school camp (in Australia) on a day-long hike, much of which was in a steep valley. I spent the first half of the hike imagining Lyndal getting herself into all sorts of dangerous situation from which I would be able to rescue her. Lyndal was the classmate I was in love with at the time. I used to fall in love a lot in high school. None of them ever fell back. That may have been because I never said anything. But my sad high school love life is not the point here.

By the time we all sat down to have a picnic lunch, I had accumulated a number of emergency situations in my imagination. Cliff-top rescues, broken bones, near-drownings. Poor Lyndal. It had been a busy morning for my brain. As everyone started to move on from lunch, a loud crack echoed around the gorge. One of our teachers had snapped her Achilles tendon when standing up. While most people kept walking once they'd worked out where the noise came from, I ran over to help. I was primed. What I had imagined had become real. Except Lyndal had been replaced by my elderly, short-sighted, American sports teacher. I joined a number of students and staff who made an impromptu stretcher and carried her back to the campsite, starting with a climb up the steep edge of the valley.

I spent many years thinking that everyone thought that way: always imagining situations that would result in a heroic intervention. To be fair, it was usually to save a girl in my case. Twenty years after not-quite-rescuing Lyndal, I found out that heroic imagination was not so common.

CHECK OUT THE SCIENCE!
Heroic Imagination

The heroic imagination is being able to imagine ourselves in heroic situations. Pretty simple, right? We've already talked about this some. But there's more. The heroic imagination also includes a "personal heroic ideal," which "can help guide a person's behavior in times of trouble or moral uncertainty" (Franco & Zimbardo, 2006, p. 31). This means the heroic imagination also includes how we think about ourselves—are we the type of person who would act heroically? We can affect this idea of ourselves by practicing—remember this?—prospection. Brain training! When you practice considering what heroic actions you could take in your own lives, you will have more self-efficacy and be more likely to act heroically if a situation calls for it. See how this all comes together?

One morning I woke up to discover that an apartment building in my complex had caught fire overnight. I immediately imagined what I would have done had the sirens woken me up. I could see myself throwing on some clothes and shoes to run over and warn everyone, perhaps even rescuing someone from their room.

Over breakfast, I discovered that my wife had a different first thought. When she heard about the fire, she imagined our daughter and me dying, followed by how she would live without us.

Later in the morning I went over to look at the building and started talking with some neighbors. One of them said she'd been worrying all morning about how she would replace all of her stuff if her building burned down.

It turns out that not everyone imagines themselves performing heroically when they see or hear about an emergency situation. And that's totally understandable! It doesn't make them bad people. But everyone can practice it. When you see a story in the news that features heroic action, ask yourself, "What would I have done?" There was even a TV show, "What Would You Do?" that creates situations using actors in public places to see how people react to situations where someone needs a hero. Hidden cameras record bystanders and heroes and then the host interviews them. In at least one episode, someone who took action said they regularly watched the show and that was the reason they had acted that way. It's an amazing example of the heroic imagination.

In 2015, Englishman Chris Norman was on a train in France. It was a common experience for him as someone who worked all across France. He had often wondered what he would do if a terror attack happened on the train. He had imagined many situations and reactions.

On that August day, he heard a gunshot and stood up to see a man at the end of the carriage holding a machine gun. His first reaction was to get on the floor behind his chair and hide. Sitting there, his mind went to his imagination sessions. He needed to do something. When he heard an American voice say, "Go get him," he joined a small team that rushed the terrorist and disabled him before anyone was killed. Chris Norman's imagination became real.

If you're not someone who is always imagining themselves performing heroic or dramatic acts, then start practicing. When you see a story of heroism online, ask yourself what you would have done in the same situation. Start a journal for this purpose. Write down the story of what you saw and then what your options would have been. If you're at the pool, think about what you could or would do if you saw someone start drowning. The more you decide what you would do before something happens, the more likely you are to do it when it does happen.

STAND OUT

One morning when I came out of my bedroom after getting dressed, my three-year-old daughter looked me up and down. Then she examined her own outfit. It was colorful, patterned, and frilly. In the way that three-year-olds do, she threw me a truth bomb. "Dad, you're boring."

She had a point. My closet contains black shirts and jeans. I've never really worn many colors and those I did wear were never bright. As I've aged, my clothing has become blacker. I just don't feel comfortable wearing colors. A daring day for me is when I wear my dark grey shirt.

I tell you this because every so often, in front of a large crowd, I wear orange pants. Not faded orange. Bright orange. I do this to feel uncomfortable. It works. It works when I step onto the stage. It works when I stop to get gas on the way to the event. I hate it. I assume that everyone looking at me is wondering why I'm dressed up for Halloween in February. But I do it because I know it's a vital part of hero training.

To be a hero, you have to be comfortable being uncomfortable. So many of the things stopping us from taking heroic action are related to being embarrassed, or fear of standing out in the crowd. If you can practice being stared at in public, you can be more ready to jump into action when you're needed.

Now, you might wear orange pants on a regular basis, so my challenge wouldn't work for you. Maybe it's dying your hair. Maybe there's nothing fashion-related that could make you uncomfortable—lucky you. Phil Zimbardo used to challenge his students at Stanford to draw a dot on their forehead and leave it on for a day. They weren't allowed to explain it or conceal it. He asked them to observe how people reacted and how it felt knowing that people were staring at you, wondering what that dot was for. You could go to the mall and walk around backwards for half an hour. You'd get plenty of stares and questions and insults. You might even get recorded and become someone's social media joke.

Once a week, make yourself uncomfortable in public. Every moment of awkwardness makes it more likely that you'll be fine taking that important step out of the crowd when the time comes. Don't make this something you do every day, though. If I wore orange pants every day, I'd get used to it. I'd be the guy who wears orange pants instead of the guy who always wears black. It would be expected and comfortable. Then I'd have to start wearing black again just to feel uncomfortable.

QUESTION THE RULES

The rules are the rules. You have to obey the law. Do what's right. That's what we're told. But what if there are different "rights"?

What's right according to the "rules" isn't always what's right in your gut. I talked about it in the Contradicting Voices section in Chapter 3. The "rules" could be laws or they could be what's expected and accepted in your community or culture—the norms. Sometimes they're just not right at all. It used to be law that Black Americans could not use certain bathrooms. It used to be law that women weren't allowed to vote. It used to be law that humans could be owned. Some people questioned those rules in countries around the world, and laws were changed to what is right. Or closer to right, anyway—there's pretty much always still work to be done.

CHECK OUT THE SCIENCE!
Red Sneakers and Nonconformity

Behaviors that go against the norm can affect how a person sees themselves and how others see them. When scientists investigated successful business people who broke the norms of their organizations, they found that people high in the social hierarchy could get away with it. They could dress, speak, and behave differently, and their high position made it so that nothing bad really happened to them.

These nonconformists were actually seen as *more* competent. Like a high-status business executive who wears a hoodie and red sneakers to work instead of a suit; coworkers might see this person as so successful and competent that they can choose to break the norms. But this only applied if people thought they were doing it on purpose! If people thought someone didn't *realize* they were breaking the norms, suddenly the message is very different—it's more like they just don't understand how to fit in, not that they're purposely challenging norms. So this all relates back to courage—it's only seen as brave (and a good thing) if it's intentional.

There are still laws in most countries that are not "right." What do we do about that?

One of the biggest rules in school is that you should never snitch. Don't be a tattle tale or you'll lose all of your friends (or so we're told). It takes a strong hero to overcome this rule when there's a serious issue that needs adult help. You could make this easier if you have a conversation with your friends about this rule. Most of them will agree that if something serious is going on that needs outside help you should try to find it, but unless this conversation has actually happened, the snitch rule generally takes priority.

Throughout all societies there are certain positions that possess the kind of authority that you don't challenge. Many of those positions have uniforms—police officers, religious leaders, soldiers, scientists. We don't expect these people would do anything wrong or tell us to do anything wrong. Unfortunately, they are all just people, so some of them will do (and ask others to do) bad things.

Stanley Milgram performed a famous psychology experiment in the early 1960s. He invited people to participate in a test on whether electric shocks would help someone learn better. Participants were asked to read out a question to a learner in another room. If the learner got the question wrong, they were given an electric shock. The shock level was increased for every question. In the same room as the participant was a man in a lab coat, the experimenter. The learner and experimenter were both actors; there was no actual electric shock. The "learner" started to scream and yell as the "shocks" got worse and at a point of extreme voltage, and eventually they went quiet. Milgram wanted to see how many people would keep shocking the learner all the way to the end: 450 volts. He wondered how much power the authority of a lab coat would have.

Milgram asked many colleagues and psychology students what they thought would happen. They figured around 0.01% would go to the end, but that the vast majority would stop before that. In the first experiment (Milgram replayed this many times with different variations) every participant went up to at least 300 volts, and 65% of them went all the way to the end. Every single participant stopped to question whether they should

CHECK OUT THE SCIENCE!
Rules and Development of Moral Values

Whistleblowers—people who call out a high-ranking person or company for wrongdoing—are usually risking their own personal peace and even safety to try to change things or get justice. Pretty heroic.

But even whistleblowers recommend courageous conversations with the person or company as the first step, instead of immediately blowing the whistle. These are difficult conversations that need to be had with peers, supervisors, and authority figures about topics like race, class, and gender when a rule, or law, or whole culture needs to change.

These conversations require passion, practice, and persistence. Passion because whatever you are trying to change will be difficult, so it needs to be something you care deeply about. Practice because you may need to take multiple steps and build multiple relationships. And persistence because this type of change usually does not happen quickly. It will likely take multiple courageous conversations, and multiple strategies to fix the problems that need to be solved.

But it can be done! Some business professionals have encouraged rebelling—being willing to question the rules and norms. These "rebels" tend to have passion, creativity, and curiosity in their work lives, and use their individual strengths, passion, talents, and creativity to work to change and improve the organizations they work for. And studies suggest that businesses that hire and support these rebel workers actually perform better than businesses who are afraid to hire "rebel" workers because they are difficult to manage!

continue shocking this poor person on the other side of the wall, but the man in a lab coat convinced them to continue.

Authority figures are capable of convincing us to do (and ignore) terrible things. It's important that you feel comfortable questioning people in positions of authority. Remember that they're humans too, and that humans can get things wrong. They might even be just following the rules of some other person with authority.

For hero training, you can start questioning the rules that seem odd to you. I don't mean rules you don't like, but rules that seem to restrict you from doing the right thing. You can do it in your head or out loud. It's safer to ask in your head of course, but heroes take risks when the risks make sense. It's important to show respect when doing this. The questioning is likely to make people feel uncomfortable and get defensive. Consider how you're asking, and you should be fine.

Ewan Drum, aged 7, had heard people say that all homeless people were "bums." He heard that you weren't supposed to enable the "addicts" and "drunks" that you see on the street by giving them money or blankets. Those were just the rules of the region. As a seven-year old, he wasn't expected to challenge the rules. Ewan saw things differently. The needs of the homeless population in Detroit were his Call to Adventure.

With a new hero name, Super Ewan, began traveling to Detroit to hand out meals and blankets. When he Crossed the Threshold into the city, from his hometown in eastern Michigan, he did so with his family. They became the first members of his Hero Team and helped throughout the Path of Trials. Along that path, he met people who joined in to hand out food and supplies as well as a few who gave him money to keep it growing. Other people he never even met donated money and told his story.

He encountered resistance when he decided to help because it's so unusual to break the rules, even when they're not officially laws. Ewan had always figured that people were people and that everyone deserved love and the basic necessities. He questioned the established rules in his community that the homeless should be left to figure things out by themselves and made a difference in the lives of thousands. With his red Super Ewan cape, he now shares what he's learned to people around the world, including Barack Obama and Michael Phelps. By doing the right thing and beginning his own hero's journey, Ewan became the Master of Two Worlds.

FIND NEW GROUPS

As discussed earlier, we're easily influenced by our social groups. We like to stick with those wearing the same colors as us, who speak our language, or look like us. A lot of these things are superficial. That makes sense because way back when your small social group was vital to your survival, you didn't have time to sit down for a conversation about things you had in common. You had to decide if this stranger wanted to steal a few hours of conversation or steal your cows.

These days your brain is capable of understanding that people who look different aren't out to get you. That's a great development for a world in which we can travel from any place to another in less than a couple of days. However, our brains still default to this old instinct when tested under stress or time constraints. Luckily, we're smarter than our brains.

Overcoming that instinct is supremely difficult and can take a long time. A really long time. But we can trick our brains by joining more groups. The more and more diverse groups you belong to, the more likely your brain is to see a connection with someone who needs your help. Your brain has a checklist. If it can quickly find something in common, then it will let you act. It might go like this: Does this person look like me? No. Do they sound like me? No. Are they wearing my team's colors? No. Have I seen them at my school? No. Are they wearing the same obscure, cool shoe brand as me? YES! Help now!

This trick can work by doing two things. One is to join new groups and the other is to think about the groups you already belong to.

Joining new groups can be intimidating, tricky, and potentially embarrassing, but it's worth trying. Every day in cafeterias across the country (and world), kids are sitting in the same groups as every other day. Some of them are even sitting in exactly the same seat every day. This is that old, instinctual behavior. Your job is to break it. Go and sit somewhere else. I grew up on American high school movies from the 80s, so I assumed sitting with a different group at lunch time would result in embarrassing and dangerous repercussions. However, I am pretty sure today's cafeterias are a bit more forgiving. It's still stressful—if it weren't, everyone would do it. Many schools have recognized how tough this is, as well as how helpful switching up groups is for a better school community, so they have Mix It Up Day when everyone sits with someone they don't usually eat lunch with.

You can also start joining other types of social groups. There are sports teams, board game clubs, artist collectives, and many more inside and outside of school. Most of these are always looking for new members, so it's a little easier than sitting with different people at school.

Examining your existing groups is useful too. Sometimes being made more aware of the groups you belong to helps you act heroically.

For example, Mark Levine, professor at the University of Exeter, ran an experiment similar to the one I described run by my wife in the social groups section from earlier. He asked Manchester United soccer fans to write an essay about why they loved their team so much. Then he asked them to walk across the campus to another room for the next part. Mark placed an actor in between the two rooms who needed help. In one test the actor wore a plain shirt, in the second a Manchester United shirt, and in the third, the shirt of Manchester's bitter rivals, Liverpool. As you can guess, the fans were more likely to help their fellow fan and least likely to help their enemy. This was not the end of the experiment though. Mark repeated the test, this time asking the Manchester United fans to write about why they loved soccer so much. The results were dramatically different. The plain-shirted person was helped less than the soccer shirts, who were helped an equal amount whether they wore Man U or Liverpool gear. An amazing change just based on what they focused their minds on. Imagine what you could do if you regularly focused on the groups—and the variations of those groups, like "soccer fan" versus "specific team fan"—you belong to.

One activity you could run starts in your classroom. Ask your teacher for ten minutes. Assign a superhero (or any other topic) to each corner in the room and then ask everyone to go to the corner for the character they like the most. Each person then has to explain in 60 seconds why they chose that corner. Ten minutes later you will know the names and faces of a new group of people with a similarity to you. When you're walking down the hall and see someone who was as big a fan of Wonder Woman as you were, and they're in need of help, you're much more likely to help them. You can repeat this more than once to discover who belongs to other groups with you.

HONOR CODE

Imagine believing in a set of rules so strongly that you'd kill yourself if you broke any of them. The samurai had such a collection. They called it Bushido. The eight tenets of Bushido, according to author, Nitobe Inazō's book *Bushido: The Soul of Japan*, were: Justice, Courage, Benevolence (Kindness), Respect, Honesty, Honor, Self-Control, and Loyalty. These words guided the actions of the samurai every day. They learned about them in school on an equal level with reading, writing, and math. They thought about how to apply them to their lives and choices. They read stories that described the code in action. And many times, if they felt they'd done something that clashed with Bushido, they killed themselves. It was that serious.

Many famous groups throughout history have had strong **honor codes** that directed them in their behavior—most of them didn't feel the need to kill themselves if they broke the code, thankfully, and neither should you. The Boy Scouts have the simple "Be Prepared" motto that directs them in everything that they do. They also have the "A scout is . . ." series of statements that state expectations. Jack Sparrow follows the Pirate Code in the Disney movies, but the pirates that inspired his creation had their own code that actually kept them very successful despite breaking the laws of national governments.

Codes remain a useful tool in today's world. When I worked for the YMCA, we had a code that directed all of our efforts and showed our customers what we expected from them. It was four words: Responsibility, Caring, Respect, and Honesty. Making these sorts of things public helps large organizations attract employees who want to follow a similar code—it's another way of joining a group.

CHECK OUT THE SCIENCE!
Don't Be Afraid to Change

What you believe and how you behave will likely change over time. That's fine; everyone is a work in progress (growth mindset!) and what's most important to you (your moral values!) may change over time. Some things that you believe are "right" today may seem less right, or even wrong, in a few years. Or the opposite—things that seem wrong now might seem right later on! Do your best to grow your empathy, social responsibility, and compassion for others, and these changes in your moral values will help you use your unique passions and talents to improve the world.

To create your own code, give some thought to the words that are most important to you. Have a look at some codes from history, from your school, and from books or movies. Write down anything that you feel is important. You'll probably get a big list. Now circle the ten that speak most powerfully to you. It might be helpful to put each word on a post-it note and arrange them in order. This could be something that takes a few days of thinking. Take a long walk and bounce the words around in your head to see which of them end up on top. As a final step, create a poster or a small, private note (whichever you prefer!) with your code and put it in a spot that you'll see every day. It could be near your mirror, on your ceiling, or in your locker.

Like many of the hero training pieces, this works because it tricks your brain into an automatic reaction. When you focus on your code on a daily basis, it digs itself into your brain. If you're reflecting on the word Honesty every morning, you're going to more honest as an automatic reaction.

∿→ PUT IT ALL TOGETHER! ←∿

Of course you can be a hero! After all we've talked about, you probably knew that already, but now you know how to put it into action. Remember:

- Practice a Heroic Habit; get in the habit of doing good. Even the smallest actions can have a big effect.

- Practice having a growth mindset. Stand out, do things that scare you, and remind yourself that if you can't do something, you can't do it *yet*. Lots of people thought they could never do something until they did it.

- Pay attention to your values, morals, and honor code. Don't be afraid to question the rules and find new groups if the actions of those around you don't seem moral or just.

Find your people, your goals, your power, and your heroic attitude, and you'll be surprised just how quickly you can . . .

LEAVE A LEGACY

When a hero becomes the Master of Two Worlds, they change the world. They share knowledge or make a difference with their actions. They leave a **legacy**.

Dorothy learns the importance of home and friendship and courage. Mulan realizes how important it is to be yourself. Katniss shows the Districts that it is possible to stand up to the Capitol. Most heroes don't think about what their legacy is going to be. Certainly, most real life people don't think about how their journeys are going to change the world. Let's face it, when the school year ends, you're thinking about getting out of there as soon as possible and moving on to summer and the next grade—not what you've left behind.

However, as an expert on the hero's journey, you may start thinking about this. How can you leave a legacy? How can you make sure people remember that you were there? Will the future students at your current school feel the impact you made?

There are two ways to go about making your presence felt by future generations. The first is to change something. What is something about your school that you think needs to be fixed? Maybe there's an issue with the dress code. Maybe there isn't enough student representation in decision making. At one school I visited, a student had successfully fought to change the way prom was organized. His name was still known by students four years later who had never met him. That is leaving a legacy.

What could you fix in the world around you before you move onto the next world? Write down some ideas and maybe discuss it with some friends tomorrow. There is still lots of time before you finish your journey. Make people remember you. Make your journey improve the world. Make your Lovelace yell out that he'll be telling your story long after you're gone.

Of course, people remembering you by name isn't the be-all and end-all of making a difference. Plenty of people have made a difference and improved the world whose names have been lost to history. Or maybe they were just notable to a few people. That doesn't make them less important. The other way to have your experience matter is to share your knowledge. As I've already said many times, the first few days on a new hero's journey are scary. Not knowing what is ahead causes that fear. Imagine if you had someone who had already finished that journey sharing everything they'd learned. What if at the end of twelfth grade a student went back to her old middle school and shared everything she knew with those eighth graders? That could be life-changing for some of them. The twelfth grader remembers what she was afraid of and she now knows what these eighth graders should actually be worrying about.

A couple of years ago I presented this idea to 300 eighth graders. Two girls from that group took it upon themselves to create a "Guide to Surviving Middle School" and went back to give a speech to all of the fifth graders at their old elementary school. These girls discussed everything that they'd learned and shared it with those about to embark on that same journey. That is priceless information. That is leaving a legacy.

Now it's your turn. Put this book down and take some time to compile your list of lessons from the last year. Create it as if you were able to get in a time machine and deliver the message to your younger self. This list should not be just what you think other people want you to say. Don't write down, "Get enough sleep, do your homework on time, and be respectful." Boring! Think about the things you actually learned. Mine from my first year of high school: "Don't go to school with your socks pulled all the way up. Don't be afraid to talk to Deena. Get enough sleep." It turns out that the sleep one *is* actually important.

Now find someone to share your list with. Help that person overcome their fear of what's to come.

BE FIRST

Have you ever stood at a crosswalk with "DON'T WALK" flashing but no cars in sight? Do you walk across, or do you stay and wait for it to turn? If there's a crowd already waiting, you probably wait because of what we talked about in The Crowd section of Chapter 3. What's interesting is when someone ignores the crowd and walks across anyway. All of a sudden other people start walking across as well. It only took one person to give them permission to act. Now, jaywalking is generally frowned upon, so this is not a recommendation. However, the power is clear and extends to heroic behavior.

How many people do you think refused to give up their seats on buses in the week after the news about Rosa Parks came out? How many people joined the #MeToo movement after the first public announcement even after years of staying silent? Going first can help others take action by showing them the way, showing them that it's okay. Your actions can spread. When you influence one person to start acting, they can inspire others. Your going first can create a tree of positive actions with branches extending in all sorts of directions.

Chad Lindsey, who I mentioned earlier, did what all emergency responder classes suggest—he asked for help. Instead of hoping someone would help lift his unconscious commuter, he asked them directly. As strange as it sounds, that gave the bystanders permission to help. Seeing Chad got them thinking that they could also do something, but what? They didn't have to imagine something to do, here was a man on the tracks asking for specific help. When you do need help, ask for something specific and ask a specific person. "Hey, you in the red coat, call 9-1-1," is much better than "Someone call for help!"

For many reasons, it's scary to go first. You might fail and get embarrassed. You might not know what to do. You might know there are negative repercussions waiting for you. But if no one acts, nothing gets done.

Someone has to go first. It might as well be you.

GLOSSARY

Action Hero: someone who takes action for the good of others, despite a risk or sacrifice.

Altruistic Behavior: actions at are unselfish, that will benefit the group but not necessarily benefit the individual.

Amygdala: a part of the brain that plays a role in fear learning and determining if something is a threat.

Assistant: the person who joins in and helps in a situation; in the example of bullying, this person will join the bully with hurtful words or actions.

Attribution Theory: how we think about other people's behavior, whether it is caused by something internal or external.

Automatic Decision Making: a type of decision making that involves no thought because a behavior or rule is repeated enough times that the brain begins to do it without thinking.

Bystander: the person who ignores a situation and allows it to happen; in the example of bullying, this person will not join in, but will not stop it either.

Bystander Effect: the name for the assumption that someone else will do what's right when you're in a group, so no one ends up taking action.

Call to Adventure: the moment the hero of a story is invited on an adventure by another character, an event, or a discovery.

Classical Conditioning: a type of learning in which a behavior is developed as a response to a stimulus.

Civic Engagement: working to better your community through action, like community service.

Empathy: the ability to put yourself in another person's shoes and understand their thoughts and feelings.

Fear Setting: the practice of examining your fears in order to overcome them.

Fixed Mindset: the belief that your abilities and personality cannot be changed or improved.

Growth Mindset: the belief that your abilities and personality can be built, strengthened, or expanded.

Hero Team: the group of people that assist a hero, whether in a fictional story or the real world.

Hero's Journey: a series of steps found in almost every hero story ever written, popularized by Joseph Campbell.

Heroic Imagination: thinking and imagining a situation in which you are acting heroic, in an effort to encourage yourself to act heroically later.

Heroic Habit: a small repeated action that can make helping others almost automatic.

Honor Code: a set of values or expectations laid out by a group or individual to make clear what is expected.

Idol: a person, usually popular, who is looked up to as an example.

Impostor Syndrome: when a person doubts their abilities to the point that they feel like they are tricking others into believing they are more qualified than they are and that this person will eventually be exposed.

Joseph Campbell: a professor who collected stories and myths from around the world and wrote extensively about the hero's journey.

Legacy: the stories and lessons you leave behind.

Little Way: the theory that performing little actions every day can be equal to one large action.

Loving-kindness Meditation: a type of meditation that develops compassion by focusing on loving yourself and expanding to loving all of humanity.

Master of Two Worlds: the moment when the hero returns to the place they started, having succeeded in the new world.

Media Literacy: accessing and evaluating multiple news sources to find accurate information and form your own opinion.

Mentor: a person with more experience (and usually years) under their belt who guides and cares for a hero.

Moral Values: things that we commonly define to be right or wrong, like rules that guide your behavior.

Mundane World: the normal, everyday world. Not necessarily boring!

Path of Trials: the part of a hero's story that involves meeting new people, overcoming challenges, and gaining knowledge.

Peer Pressure: the feeling of needing to do what those around you are doing or telling you to do.

Prospection: thinking and imagining a future situation or interaction and coming up with possible outcomes.

Reaction Hero: an Action Hero who has no time to think about their actions because someone needs help RIGHT NOW!

Real Cool: the kind of cool that comes from never trying to be cool. It's a paradox.

Reinforcer: the person who encourages a situation; in the example of bullying, this person will laugh at what the bully is doing, stand and watch, or repeats the event to others.

Resiliency: the ability to adapt to new situations and bounce back after a challenge.

Round Table: from King Arthur's round table, the idea of having a group of people tackle a problem at a table where no one has the "head seat" at the table.

Self-efficacy: the belief in yourself and your ability to succeed.

Social Hierarchies: a separation between people within a group based on perceived importance, like a social ladder; those at the top are seen as authority figures.

Social Norms: behaviors that we think the group expects or prefers based on actions of others in the group.

Threshold: the entryway for the hero to the new world—can be metaphorical or a literal door or gate.

Threshold Guardians: someone (or something) that helps or hinders the hero at the entry to the new world, teaching a lesson in the process.

BIBLIOGRAPHY

CHAPTER 1:

Australian Storytelling. (1998). Pauline McLeod, NSW—
Aboriginal Perspective [Interview]. Retrieved from:
http://www.australianstorytelling.org.au/interviews/
pauline-mcleod-nsw-aboriginal-perspective

Campbell, J. (1949). *The hero with a thousand faces*. Pantheon Books.

Gladwell, M. (2002). *The tipping point: How little things can make
a big difference*. Back Bay Books.

Macrae, C. N., & Bodenhausen, G. V. (2000). Social cognition:
Thinking categorically about others. *Annual Review of
Psychology, 51*, 93–120.

Todorov, A. (2017). *Face value: The irresistible influence of first
impressions*. Princeton University Press.

CHAPTER 2:

Joseph Campbell Foundation. [Quote]. Retrieved from:
https://www.jcf.org/works/quote/we-have-not-even-to-risk/

Pajares, F. (2006). Self-efficacy during childhood and adolescence.
Self-efficacy beliefs of adolescents, 5, 339–367.

Schunk, D. H., & Meece, J. L. (2005). Self-efficacy development in adolescence. *Self-efficacy beliefs of adolescents*, 5, 71–96.

Seneca, L. A. (1969). *Letters from a stoic*. Penguin Books.

CHAPTER 3:

Arendt, H. (1981). *The life of the mind*. Houghton Mifflin Harcourt.

Asch S. E. (1956). Studies of independence and conformity: I. A minority of one against a unanimous majority. *Psychological Monographs*, 70, 1–70.

Belman, J., & Flanagan, M. (2010). Designing games to foster empathy. *International Journal of Cognitive Technology*, 15(1), 11.

Berkowitz, M. W. (1997). The complete moral person: Anatomy and formation. In J. DuBois (Ed.), *Moral Issues in Psychology* (pp. 11–41). University Press of America, Inc.

Bloom, S. G. (September 2005). Lesson of a lifetime. *Smithsonian Magazine*. Retrieved from: https://www.smithsonianmag.com/science-nature/lesson-of-a-lifetime-72754306/

Brown, R. M. (1984). *Unexpected news: Reading the Bible with third world eyes*. Westminster John Knox Press.

Corredor, J. M. (1956). *Conversations with casals*. Dutton.

Damon, W., & Colby, A. (2015). *The power of ideals: The real story of moral choice*. Oxford University Press, USA.

Fischer, P., Krueger, J. I., Greitemeyer, T., Vogrincic, C., Kastenmüller, A., Frey, D., Heene, M., Wicher, M., & Kainbacher, M. (2011). The bystander-effect: A meta-analytic review on bystander intervention in dangerous and non-dangerous emergencies. *Psychological Bulletin*, 137(4), 517.

Manning, R., Levine, M., & Collins, A. (2007). The Kitty Genovese murder and the social psychology of helping: The parable of the 38 witnesses. *American Psychologist, 62*(6), 555.

Milgram, S. (1963). Behavioral study of obedience. *The Journal of abnormal and social psychology, 67*(4), 371.

Ng, C. (2017, January 19). 20 small acts of resistance to make your voice heard over the next 4 years: Protest injustice and make the world a better place. Retrieved from: https://www.teenvogue.com/story/20-small-acts-of-resistance

Seligman, M. E., Railton, P., Baumeister, R. F., & Sripada, C. (2013). Navigating into the future or driven by the past. *Perspectives on Psychological Science, 8*(2), 119–141.

Wiesel, E. (1986, December 10). *Elie Wiesel—Acceptance speech*. The Nobel Prize. Retrieved from: https://www.nobelprize.org/prizes/peace/1986/wiesel/26054-elie-wiesel-acceptance-speech-1986/

Wren, C. S. (1991, August 5). Over 500 Are Rescued as Greek Cruise Ship Sinks Off South African Coast. *The New York Times*. Retrieved from: https://www.nytimes.com/1991/08/05/world/over-500-are-rescued-as-greek-cruise-ship-sinks-off-south-african-coast.html

Zimbardo, P. (2007). The Lucifer effect: Understanding how good people turn evil. New York. Random House.

CHAPTER 4:

Malory, T. (1998). *Le Morte D'arthur: The Winchester manuscript* (H. Cooper, Ed.). Oxford University Press.

Ohio State University. (2012, May 7). 'Losing yourself' in a fictional character can affect your real life. *ScienceDaily*. Retrieved from: www.sciencedaily.com/releases/2012/05/120507131948.htm

Wilson, M. (2009, March 17). Leap to Track. Rescue Man. Clamber Up. Catch a Train. *The New York Times*. Retrieved from: https://www.nytimes.com/2009/03/18/nyregion/18subway.html

CHAPTER 5:

Neil Gaiman: Keynote Address 2012. (2012, May 17). University of the Arts. Retrieved from: https://www.uarts.edu/neil-gaiman-keynote-address-2012

Orwell, G. (1945). *Animal farm*. Secker and Warburg.

CHAPTER 6:

Faris, R., & Felmlee, D. (2011). Status struggles: Network centrality and gender segregation in same-and cross-gender aggression. *American Sociological Review, 76*(1), 48–73.

Gray, G. (Personal communication, August 5, 2019).

Kim, E. K. (2013, January 8). Teen uses tweets to compliment his classmates. *Today.com*. Retrieved from: https://www.today.com/news/teen-uses-tweets-compliment-his-classmates-flna1B7882246

McDaniel, I. (2012, January 13). Friendship found in unexpected places. *My Jag News*. Retrieved from: https://newspaper.neisd.net/johnson/2012/01/31/friendship-found-in-unexpected-places/

Parker-Pope, T. (2011, February 14). Web of popularity, achieved by bullying. *The New York Times*. Retrieved from: https://well.blogs.nytimes.com/2011/02/14/web-of-popularity-weaved-by-bullying/

Pink Shirt Day. (n.d.). Retrieved from: https://www.pinkshirtday.ca/about

CHAPTER 7:

Anderson, J. (2015, July 29). How a small-time drug dealer rescued dozens during Katrina. *Buzzfeed*. Retrieved from: https://www.buzzfeed.com/joelanderson/how-a-small-time-drug-dealer-rescued-dozens-during-katrina

Bellezza, S., Gino, F., & Keinan, A. (2014). The red sneakers effect: Inferring status and competence from signals of nonconformity. *Journal of Consumer Research*, 41(1), 35–54.

Children's Day 2019: Motivational quotes by Jawaharlal Nehru. (2019, November 14). *The Times of India*. Retrieved from: https://timesofindia.indiatimes.com/home/education/news/childrens-day-2019-motivational-quotes-by-jawaharlal-nehru/articleshow/72042336.cms

Condon, P., Desbordes, G., Miller, W. B., & DeSteno, D. (2013). Meditation increases compassionate responses to suffering. *Psychological Science*, 24(10), 2125–2127.

Dweck, C. S. (2008). *Mindset: The new psychology of success*. Random House Digital, Inc.

Edwardes, D. (2016, January 13). Undoing the architecture of fear. *DanEdwardes.com*. Retrieved from: https://danedwardes.com/2016/01/23/undoing-the-architecture-of-fear/

Ferris, T. (2017, May 15). Fear setting: The most valuable exercise I do every month [Blog post]. Retrieved from: https://tim.blog/2017/05/15/fear-setting/

Franco, Z. E., & Zimbardo, P. G. (2006). The banality of heroism. *Greater Good*, 3(2), 30–35.

Gino, F. (2018). *Rebel talent: Why it pays to break the rules at work and in life*. Pan Macmillan.

Keating, S., & Biddle, N. (2015, August 27.) Oh my God, it's happening: 62-year-old man who helped American train heroes recalls 20 minutes of terror aboard the Thalys. *People*. Retrieved from: https://people.com/human-interest/chris-norman-reveals-heroic-role-in-paris-train-attack/

Langford, J., & Clance, P. R. (1993). The imposter phenomenon: Recent research findings regarding dynamics, personality and family patterns and their implications for treatment. *Psychotherapy: Theory, Research, Practice, Training*, 30(3), 495.

Levine, M., Prosser, A., Evans, D., & Reicher, S. (2005). Identity and emergency intervention: How social group membership and inclusiveness of group boundaries shape helping behavior. *Personality and Social Psychology Bulletin*, 31(4), 443–453. https://doi.org/10.1177/0146167204271651

Mansfield, K. C., & Jean-Marie, G. (2015). Courageous conversations about race, class, and gender: Voices and lessons from the field. *International Journal of Qualitative Studies in Education*, 28(7), 819–841.

Martin, G. R. R. (1996). *A game of thrones*. Bantam Spectra.

Milgram, S. (1963). Behavioral study of obedience. *The Journal of Abnormal and Social Psychology*, 67(4), 371–378. https://doi.org/10.1037/h0040525

Nucci, L., & Narvaez, D. (2014). Introduction and Overview. In *Handbook of Moral and Character Education* (pp. 17–24). Routledge.

Pletcher, K. (2019, September 9). Bushidō. *Encyclopædia Britannica*. Retrieved from: https://www.britannica.com/topic/Bushido

Roskowski, J. C. R. (2010). *Imposter phenomenon and counseling self-efficacy: The impact of imposter feelings* (Doctoral dissertation, Ball State University).

Sakulku, J., & Alexander, J. (2011). The impostor phenomenon. *The Journal of Behavioral Science*, 6(1), 75–97.

Steinberg, S. (2017, May 9). 'Super Ewan' helps the homeless in Detroit. *The Detroit News*. Retrieved from: https://www.detroitnews.com/story/news/local/detroit-city/2017/05/09/super-ewan-helps-homeless-detroit/101454214/

Teaching Tolerance. (n.d.). Mix-It-Up. Retrieved from: https://www.tolerance.org/mix-it-up

MATT LANGDON is the founder of the Hero Construction Company, creator of the Hero Round Table (the world's leading conference on heroism), and a board member of Dr. Philip Zimbardo's Heroic Imagination Project. He speaks to audiences around the globe. He lives with his wife and daughter in a small town in southeast Australia.

Visit mattlangdon.com

🐦@TheHeroCC

BRIAN RICHES is a Doctoral Student in Positive Developmental Psychology. He is an instructor at Salt Lake Community College, and a Project Manager at the Fostering Purpose Project.

MAGINATION PRESS is the children's book imprint of the American Psychological Association. APA works to advance psychology as a science and profession and as a means of promoting health and human welfare. Magination Press books reach young readers and their parents and caregivers to make navigating life's challenges a little easier. It's the combined power of psychology and literature that makes a Magination Press book special.

Visit maginationpress.org

📘🐦📷📌@MaginationPress